Footholds & Strongholds

Discerning and Destroying

The Works of the Enemy

and

Winning the Battle for Your

Heart and Mind

David Holdaway

Copyright © David Holdaway 2015

First edition   2015

Second edition   2017

E-mail: davidholdaway1@aol.com

www.lifepublications.org.uk

Cover design by Graeme Moodie

ISBN 978-1-907929-61-8

Whatever we become dependent upon
has the power to control us

Dedication

To all those who wisely and lovingly
minister deliverance and healing in Jesus' Name

Contents

Foreword

Rochester Castle and the Pigs!

Nestled between London and mainland France, the city of Rochester was an important strategic spot for defence and communication. As a result, it was one of the very first castles ever to be built in England around 1066, just after the Norman invasion. The sheer might of Rochester Castle's stone tower meant that it could easily withstand attacks and sieges.

In 1215, not long after the signing of the Magna Carta, King John attacked the castle because his barons reneged on their agreement to hand the fortress over to his control. Arriving on October 13 the king's forces began to pelt the stronghold's walls with huge stones and ammunition from their trebuchet siege-engines.

Towards the end of that month, King John's forces managed to burrow under the surrounding curtain wall but the stronghold was made of stern stuff. Despite pelting it with vast rocks, it stood firm. So the king then tried mining under the south-west corner in order to collapse the outer defences, but this was also unsuccessful.

King John had one more trick up his sleeve. On November 25 his commanders wrote to London requesting "forty of the fattest pigs, the sort least good for eating". Why such pigs? Because before gun-powder, pig-fat was used as an explosive and as a fire-starter.

The pig-fat created a fire strong enough to burn through the mine-shaft beneath the tower, and collapse part of the castle. This was the beginning of the end for the mighty fortress. By early December, the remaining rebels inside were near-starved and exhausted, and surrendered to the King.

The strategy of lighting fires under castle walls became an important weapon in the besieging army's arsenal to collapse the foundations of the stronghold.

When dealing with spiritual strongholds one of the most powerful ways to see them demolished is by lighting a fire under their fortifications. The fire of the Holy Spirit can burn through the buttresses and ramparts of any addiction and bondage.

There is an invisible spiritual war going on all around us and in this conflict there is no neutrality or Geneva Convention. It is an all out battle between the forces of evil and the Kingdom of God. The good news is that Satan has already been defeated through the death and resurrection of Jesus and as His followers we do not fight to achieve conquest but to enforce a victory already won.

Most people in the devil's kingdom do not realise they are a part of it because it is a kingdom of darkness and they can't see it. Conversely, God's kingdom is a kingdom of light and those who are in it know they are.

When describing how Satan's kingdom is to be defeated Jesus gave us the principle of *binding the strongman*, Matthew 12:29. This ruler has control of the place he occupies and makes it his stronghold. Jesus tells us that simply attacking it and gaining an entrance is not enough, we have to *bind the strongman to plunder his goods.*

In Matthew 16:18,19, Jesus says to Peter,

> *I tell you that you are Peter, and on this rock I will build my church, and the gates of Hades will not overcome it. I will give you the keys of the kingdom of heaven; whatever you bind on earth will be bound in heaven, and whatever you loose on earth will be loosed in heaven.*

"Binding" and "loosing" were common terms used by the Rabbis in biblical times. When the Rabbis "bound" something, they "forbade" it, and when they "loosed" something, they "permitted" it. Jesus is saying to His church that He has given us authority to oppose and prohibit the work of the kingdom of darkness and power to release the rule and reign of God upon the earth.

As you read the following pages my prayer is that you will experience God's Kingdom come and His will done in every area of your life and that you may be a carrier of His Kingdom to others.

David Holdaway

Footholds and Strongholds

Introduction

The Gollum Effect

*Today's Idol Will Become
Tomorrow's Master*

The country of Wales, in which I live, has the distinction of having more castles than anywhere else in the world for both its geographical size and population. There are more than 600 of these stronghold fortresses, mostly built by invading forces to capture and rule the people and the land. They were strategically sited for maximum control and command. The same is true of spiritual powers that are constantly looking for footholds to build strongholds in people's lives.

In the films and the book *The Lord of the Rings,* the tragic character of Gollum is portrayed as someone who has become totally captured and consumed by "The Ring of Power."

As soon as he sees the ring it draws him and he must have it and kills to do so. It now belongs to Gollum, but the more he is captivated with it, the more he is captured by it. He does not have the ring but rather the power of the ring possesses him, and his life and destiny become bound to and destroyed by it. What started as an attraction ends up in his destruction.

There comes a tipping point when what we think we control starts controlling us. When this happens people keep doing something even though they know it is destroying their health, their family, and their testimony. It's frequently why those with power crave more power and do all they can to keep it and find it impossible to let go. It can be the reason rich people want more and more money and become terrified of losing what they have. It's often how a person becomes enticed by lust and is then entrenched in it. Footholds become strongholds.

High Places

In his book *Reflections,* my good friend John Lancaster talks about the ungodly places of footholds and strongholds that operated in Old Testament times, where they are referred to as *"The High Places".* He writes,

> There is a seven word sentence that punctuates and pollutes the history of the kings of Judah and Israel, on at least seven occasions these ominous words echo across the pages of the Old Testament. *"Nevertheless the high places were not removed."*

> These "high places" stood for compromise and
> demonic influence and control. They challenged
> the "sole rights" of Jehovah and became places
> of gross immorality and idolatry. (Jeremiah
> 3:1-10).

These high places in the Old Testament were left-overs from
the Canaanite religion. Whereas today's high places are most
often the areas where the old life of the flesh still claims our
allegiance. Our own sinful nature still wars against the Spirit, as
Paul reminds us in Galatians 5:17-21. The high places are areas
where we conform to the prevailing attitudes of the world
around us, its values and lifestyle. The Apostle John describes it
as the *"lust of the eyes and the pride of life,"* (1 John 2:16).

> *They angered him with their high places; they*
> *aroused his jealousy with their idols.*

Psalm 78:58

The "High Places" the enemy possesses become the low places
of pain and bondage in people's lives. Jesus came *"to destroy*
all the works of the devil," (1 John 3:8) and for every high thing
that exalts itself against the knowledge of God to be taken
captive to Himself, (2 Corinthians 10:5.)

Footholds and Strongholds

1

He Redeems my Life from the Pit

Psalm 103:4

*Jesus Christ came into the world to make
bad people good and dead people live*

Both my father and grandfather were coal miners, like many others in the South Wales valleys where I grew up. They worked in the coal pits digging out the black gold that fired the power stations and machinery of industry. The mines were dangerous places when they worked there in the 1950s and 60s but were vastly improved from generations before. They were dark, damp and gloomy and my father almost died in an accident which left him in hospital for more than a year.

At the end of every miner's work-shift the men headed for the showers at the pithead baths, their faces black and bodies bruised and cut from another battle with the coal face below. Water and soap now flowed freely as they washed and scrubbed away the dirt and coal dust. This was a safe place, no danger of explosion or a sudden cave-in or poisonous gas, they were out of the pit but they still had to cleanse the pit off themselves.

It was the same when the Israelites came out of Egypt after 400 years of slavery and bondage. The people constantly grumbled against God and Moses and spoke of how life had been better in Egypt. A whole generation died in the wilderness because even though they had come out of Egypt (the pit), Egypt had not come out of them. A journey that should have taken just eleven days to the Promised Land of Canaan took more than forty years and a million funerals.

The Three "Tenses" of Salvation

The story is told of a student at Cambridge University who approached the Professor of Divinity at the time, Brooke Foss Westcott, and asked him if he was saved.

"Ah," said Westcott, "a very good question. But tell me, what do you mean by saved?" He then went on to mention three passive participles of the Greek verb "to save", indicating that his answer would depend on which of the three the student had in mind. "I know I have been saved," he said. "I believe I am being saved, and I hope by the grace of God that I shall be saved."

When some well-meaning person asks if you are "saved" they usually mean have you repented of your sins and believe in Jesus as your Lord and Saviour. It's a good question, but what is often not understood that Professor Westcott was pointing out, is that "saved" and "salvation" is not only about what God has done but also what He is currently doing and will do in the future.

To be "saved" in scripture, therefore, is described in three tenses, "having been saved," "being saved" and "will be saved," past, present and future; and all three are part of God's redemptive work in our lives. To be redeemed means not only to be rescued but to be fully restored. John Newton, the former slave trader who wrote the hymn *Amazing Grace,* put it like this,

> "I am not what I ought to be, I am not what I want to be, I am not what I hope to be in another world; but still I am not what I once used to be, and by the grace of God I am what I am."

Dealing with the Past – Justification

When C.S.Lewis, was answering questions on the BBC radio programme *The Brains Trust*, he was once asked, "What has God to give us that no one else can give us?" He responded with one word, "Forgiveness".

Through repentance and faith in Jesus we are declared righteous by God on the basis of Christ's righteousness. At this moment we are *"Born again"* (John 3:3), and not simply given a new start in life but a new life in Christ to start with. We become a *"New creation, the old has gone and the new has come,"* 2 Corinthians 5:17. This is why justification is often described as "just as if I never sinned".

> *For it is by grace you have been saved, through faith and this not from yourselves, it is the gift of God.*
>
> Ephesians 2:8

Dealing with the Present – Sanctification

Sanctification simply means that we are set apart for a special purpose. In justification the penalty of sin is dealt with and we are declared righteous and in being sanctified the power of sin is overcome and we are being made holy. This is a process in which we cooperate with the work of the Holy Spirit to become more like Jesus.

> *The word of the cross is to them that perish foolishness; but unto us who are saved* (*being saved* – the Greek participle is in the present tense, and denotes those being saved) *it is the power of God.*

1 Corinthians 1:18

It is with reference to this present tense of salvation that Paul says, *"Work out your own salvation with fear and trembling,"* Philippians 2:12. We do not work *for* our salvation but we are told to "work it out." We are not saved *by* good works but we are saved *to do* good works.

Dealing with the Future – Glorification

> *Since we have now been justified by his blood, how much more shall we be saved from God's wrath through him!*

Romans 5:9

> *The hour has come for you to wake up from your slumber, because our salvation is nearer now than when we first believed.*

Romans 13:11

This future salvation has to do mainly with the body and deliverance from the very presence of sin. It is what the apostle

Paul is referring to when he describes the Christian's new resurrected body and when death the final enemy is destroyed,

> *When the perishable has been clothed with the imperishable, and the mortal with immortality, then the saying that is written will come true: "Death has been swallowed up in victory." "Where, O death, is your victory? Where, O death, is your sting?" The sting of death is sin, and the power of sin is the law. But thanks be to God! He gives us the victory through our Lord Jesus Christ.*
>
> 1 Corinthians 15:54 -57

Our glorification is also described by the apostle John when he tells us what the new heaven and new earth will be like (Revelation 21 and 22) and says, *"There is no more curse"* and *"No more death."*

This is a brief outline of the theological explanation of "Salvation" but what does all this mean in practice each day in our lives? It simply means God has not finished with us yet. God loved us as we were but loves us too much to leave us that way.

It also shows us that it is possible to be forgiven from sin's penalty but still be under its influence and control in certain areas of our lives. These are the places where the enemy seeks footholds to build strongholds.

It also tells us we need to understand God's cleansing as well as His forgiveness. We can be forgiven for what has happened but still feel condemned, tormented and controlled by it.

The Apostle John writing to Christians says,

> *But if we walk in the light, as he is in the light, we have fellowship with one another, and the blood of Jesus, his Son, purifies us from all sin. If we claim to be without sin, we deceive ourselves and the truth is not in us. If we confess our sins, he is faithful and just and will forgive us our sins and purify us from all unrighteousness.*
>
> 1 John 1:7-9

The Greek for the word *purifies* is in the present continuous tense, which means it goes on cleansing. There is no sin or bondage more powerful than the blood of Jesus and His blood will never lose its power.

Charles Wesley understood the significance of this when he wrote in his great hymn, *O For A Thousand Tongues To Sing*, where he declares that Jesus is able to not only deal with the penalty of our sin but also break the power of sin that has already been cancelled and forgiven.

> **He breaks the power of cancelled sin,**
> He sets the prisoner free.
> His blood can make the foulest clean:
> His blood avail'd for me.

Another great hymn writer, Augustus Toplady, wrote,

> Rock of Ages, cleft for me,
> Let me hide myself in Thee;
> Let the water and the blood,
> From Thy riven side which flowed,
> **Be of sin the double cure,**
> **Save me from its guilt and power.**

The shed blood of Jesus points not just to His death, where He gave His life for us but also to His life (*"the life is in the blood"*, Leviticus 17:11) where He gives His life to us. He is therefore not only able to deliver us from sin's penalty but also from its power and its presence.

This is why the cross and the resurrection of Jesus are inseparable. At Calvary He gives His life for us and because of His resurrection He is able to give His life to us. Only by both are we able to be saved from the penalty, power and presence of sin. It is why the apostle Paul says,

> *And if Christ has not been raised, our preaching is useless and so is your faith... And if Christ has not been raised, your faith is futile; you are still in your sins... If only for this life we have hope in Christ, we are to be pitied more than all men. But Christ has indeed been raised from the dead.*

1 Corinthians 14:17-20

The writer to the Hebrews puts it like this,

> *But because Jesus lives forever, he has a permanent priesthood. Therefore he is able to save completely those who come to God through him, because he always lives to intercede for them.*
> Hebrews 7:24,25

Jesus is presented in the book of Hebrews as both the sacrifice and the High Priest. His intercession being referred to here is not His prayers but His living presence.

By His death He is our testator, the maker of God's will and testament, and through His resurrected life He is the executor of it, the one who puts it into full effect. This is why the writer says Jesus is able to save completely, past, present and future. It also means that because He lives forever, His blood can never lose its power.

2

Spiritual Footholds

If you invite the devil to supper
he is sure to bring his pyjamas

In his play *Macbeth*, Shakespeare has the title character and his friend, Banquo, returning from battle and meeting three witches who hail Macbeth as a future King of Scotland. At first Macbeth is shaken by this greeting and then intrigued by their predictions. Banquo warns about heeding such dark prophecy as Shakespeare pens some of his most profound words regarding the motives of the powers of darkness,

> "...'tis strange;
> And oftentimes, to win us to our harm,
> The instruments of darkness tell us truths,
> Win us with honest trifles, to betray us
> In deepest consequence."

In the play Macbeth becomes increasingly captivated by the possibility of becoming the nation's ruler, and the more he harbours such ambitions the more he plots how to make it happen. Finally, it drives him to murder the reigning monarch, King Duncan, and to take his throne.

He pays a great price, however, and becomes tormented by guilt and fear. Having taken the crown by murder he has to keep it by more monstrous acts. He hires men to kill his best friend, Banquo. He seeks to have Banquo's son assassinated but he manages to escape. Macbeth rules, like all dictators, with terror and deception but is unable to enjoy what he had craved so much. In the end he is punished for his crimes and the rightful heir becomes king.

What started as a chance encounter with a group of witches turned into a reign of death, terror and a tragic end. The temptation of their prediction was the foothold in Macbeth's mind that became a stronghold in his heart.

This is how the devil operates; he is always looking for footholds in order to build strongholds. It's been said that if you give him an inch he will want to become your "ruler". More humorously it's been expressed, "If you invite the devil to supper he will always bring his pyjamas."

This can be seen tragically worked out in the life of Richard Nixon who was the only American President forced to resign from office. The tape recordings he took in his office revealed to Congress and the world his role in the cover-up of the "Watergate" scandal. These tapes also revealed an immense scope of crimes and abuses that predated the Watergate break-in of 1972. They included campaign fraud, political espionage and sabotage, illegal break-ins, improper tax audits, illegal wiretapping on a massive scale and a secret slush fund laundered in Mexico to pay those who conducted these operations. He was a president who would do anything to gain and stay in power.

Significantly, more than thirty years before while a law student at Duke University, Nixon, along with two friends broke into the Dean's office to learn what their academic standing was which would affect their future prospects. They were caught and were fortunate not to be expelled. But the "foothold" of "break in and deceit" became established at Duke long before the "stronghold" of the lust for power that led to Watergate.

One of America's most notorious serial killers was Ted Bundy. He murdered, raped and committed necrophilia (sex with his dead victims). By the time he was caught he had killed at least twenty-eight young women and girls in acts too horrible to mention. He was finally convicted and sentenced to death for killing a twelve-year-old girl and dumping her body in a pigsty.

He was executed in 1989, but before he went to the electric chair he gave a series of interviews to Dr James Dobson, founder of *Focus on the Family*.

In a final interview just hours before his execution, Bundy described the power of his addiction to pornography. He went back to his roots, explaining the development of his compulsive behaviour, revealing how his addiction to hard-core pornography began as a young boy of about 12 years finding some "soft porn" magazines outside a local grocery store. This progressed to his compulsion for increasingly hard core and violent porn which later fuelled the terrible crimes he committed. He said,

> Once you become addicted to it, and I look at this as a kind of addiction, you look for more potent, more explicit, more graphic kinds of material. Like an addiction, you keep craving

> something which is harder and gives you a
> greater sense of excitement, until you reach the
> point where the pornography only goes so far –
> that jumping off point where you begin to think
> maybe actually doing it will give you that which
> is just beyond reading about it and looking at it.

During the interview Bundy quoted the FBI's study of serial killers revealing that the most common interest among them was pornography. He referred to their report in 1986 that concluded 81 percent of serial killers were exposed to pornography at a young age.

Tragically, it's not only on death row in a maximum security cell that pernicious pornography struts its power and control. While statistics are difficult to quantify because of the massive usage of the internet, it is estimated that approximately 12 percent of all websites on the internet are pornographic and about 25 percent of downloads are related to pornography. Also, some two and a half billion emails each day have pornographic content.

A recent survey by the Barna Research Society in America revealed the devastating effects of porn plague among church goers there. It stated that only three percent of Christian men say they never view porn and that 18 percent of them view it several times a month.

Judgement

Have you ever wondered why in the Old Testament God's judgements sometimes seem so severe? When you read how the Israelites were told to go into Canaan and in some regions to destroy whole cities, it can confuse and appal us. Surely this cannot be the same God who so loved the world that He gave

His own son to die on a cross? This must surely be some scribal error or false inclusion in the text? Various theories are used to explain it away or attack the Bible and belief in God. So how do we respond?

First, we need to understand that sinful behaviour is not only personally destructive but it has a corporate dimension which opens the door to demonic powers over communities, cities and even nations.

Mel Gibson's film, *Apocalypto,* tells the story of a jungle tribe in South America which is brutally attacked, murdered and taken captive to be offered as human sacrifice by their captors to their Mayan gods. The Mayan warriors are evil, fierce and brutal and their lifestyle and practices horrific. They were without mercy or conscience. There have been many societies and peoples like this throughout history and children born into such communities became influenced and infected by the evil around them. Watching the film reminded me that the practices shown were similar to many of the tribes in the land of Canaan that God's people were warned about.

Archaeology gives some insights about what the Canaanites did. On one of their High Places, archaeologists found several stone pillars and great numbers of jars containing the remains of new-born babies. When a new house was built, a child would be sacrificed and its body built into the wall to bring good luck to the rest of the family. The firstborn were often sacrificed to Molech, a giant hollow bronze image in which a fire was built. Parents would place their children in its red hot hands and the babies would roll down into the fire. The sacrifice was invalid if the mother showed grief. She was commanded to dance and sing as the act took place. The

Israelites later copied this practice in a valley near Jerusalem called Gehenna, where hundreds of jars containing infant bones have been found. Jesus used this place to describe what hell was like.

There was also a great deal of sexual perversion and cruelty among the Canaanites. They believed that cultic prostitution was important to encourage their gods, Baal and Ashtoreth, to mate so that the land would be fertile and rain would come. Sexual diseases were rampant. Many young people forced into prostitution were abused to the point of death. Even the surrounding pagan nations were appalled by such Canaanite practices.

God gave the Canaanites 400 years to change their ways while Israel was in Egypt and after the Israelites passed through the Red Sea He waited 40 more years while Israel wandered in the wilderness.

Families who wished could have migrated out of the land and settled in nearby areas. God said repeatedly that He would drive out the inhabitants of the land before Israel and those who wished to leave had time and opportunity. The point was to destroy the evil Canaanite culture and its demonic activities rather than the individual Canaanite people. Only those who stubbornly refused to leave and continued their brutal demonic practices were destroyed with military force. Later in the Bible Canaanite individuals – such as Uriah the Hittite – show up as righteous characters.

Footholds

The city of Ephesus was the market place of Asia; it has been described as the Vanity Fair of the ancient world. It had a very prosperous banking centre with a great vault in the Temple of

Diana, which was considered the safest place in Asia Minor. Diana was the patron of all prostitutes and was depicted as a many bosomed image representing fertility and sexuality. The city was also known all over the world for its talismans, magical books and charms for which large sums were paid. We read in Acts 19 that as God moved in the city, many came to faith in Christ and a number who had practised sorcery and witchcraft brought their occult scrolls together and burned them publicly.

It's not surprising therefore, that Paul warns the Ephesian Christians about occultic powers and how they operate. He begins by telling them to beware of demonic footholds that the devil seeks to establish in their lives and church.

> *In your anger do not sin. Do not let the sun go down while you are still angry, and do not give the devil a foothold.*

Ephesians 4:26, 27

The word used for foothold is the Greek word *topos*. (We get our English word topography from it, meaning the study of land.) Paul is warning us not to give the devil any place of influence and presence in our lives. A little later in Ephesians 6 we have one of the clearest descriptions of spiritual warfare in the whole Bible and the need to *"Put on the whole armour of God to take our stand against the devil's schemes."*

Significantly, it is in the context of the need to live godly lives that Paul also warns us about the power of spiritual footholds and the danger of anger and nursing our wrath (*"do not let the sun go down when you are still angry,"* Ephesians 4:26).

There is a godly anger that is controlled and aroused by evil and injustice. Ungodly anger, however, tends to either simmer, plotting its revenge, or erupts and strikes out uncontrollably. It is this kind of anger that gives the devil a "foothold" because it opens the door to dangerous thoughts and emotions.

The first occurrence of such anger in the Bible is in Genesis 4 where Cain is jealous that his brother Abel's sacrifice has been accepted by God and his own has been rejected. Cain is furious and boiling over with anger, it shows in his face. God asks him why he is so downcast and warns Cain that *"sin is crouching at the door"* and if he does not master it he will be consumed by it.

Cain had given the devil a foothold, and instead of heeding God's warning he yielded to his own envy and hatred which eventually drove him to murder his brother. As a result of this he became an outcast and a wanderer who would never find peace.

We do not reap what we *sin*. If we deal with it quickly then it is cleansed and has no power within or over us. But we do definitely reap what we *sow*; what we allow to take hold and become a part of us will bear fruit whether it is good or evil.

In his book *Though I Speak with Tongues*, one of America's most respected Christian leaders, Jack Hayford, tells of one of the greatest battles in his spiritual life. He says it took place at a time after he had made his deepest commitment to move in the realm of the Spirit's fullness.

> Early in my ministry, though my marriage was strong and my commitment to Christ was solid, I slowly but definitely began to find

myself in an emotional entrapment. My involvement with a woman of equal dedication evolved into an affinity that in time moved from friendship to a near-adulterous infatuation.

During those dark days of a temptation to which I never surrendered, I wrestled long in prayer against the emotional tentacles seeking to drag me into sin. I would often cry out to God, frequently with surges of the spiritual language gushing forth in intercession for my own helplessness. It is to the praise of God's grace that I was spared the loss of my integrity, my marriage, my ministry, my life!

It was a battle he won against dark spiritual forces and the lusts of his own flesh. The enemy sought to gain a foothold but Hayford, by God's grace and his spiritual passion to fight for his own heart, resisted and rejected the invader.

But how do footholds develop into strongholds? And what do you do when strongholds have become established? That's what we are going to deal with in the next few chapters.

Footholds and Strongholds

3

How Footholds Become Strongholds

The Devil is always looking for a
Foothold to build a Stronghold

It's easier to deal with a cold than pneumonia.
It's easier to deal with a thought than an attitude.
It's easier to deal with a spill than a stain.
It's easier to deal with a foothold than a stronghold.

Something was clearly not right with David. Maybe he was tired and depressed, or simply life and battle fatigue had caught up with him. Even though he was king and loved and admired, perhaps those times of loneliness and fear of being hunted like an animal when he was younger had left their scars. Or it could just have been the lust of his desires that rose within him and overwhelmed his conscience and the voice of God. Whatever the reason it was first revealed by him choosing the comfort and safety of the palace instead of leading his army onto the battlefield.

> *In the spring, at the time when kings go off to war, David sent Joab out with the king's men and the whole Israelite army. They*

destroyed the Ammonites and besieged
Rabbah. But David remained in Jerusalem.

1 Samuel 11:1

It was spring in the nation but winter in David's soul.

There is nothing wrong with the rest and pleasure of the palace lawns, indeed we all need those times of refreshing and renewing, the problems arose, however, not so much because of where David was physically but because of what was happening within him emotionally and spiritually.

As he walked the palace grounds something caught his eye, no, it was someone. He saw one of the most dangerous sights known to man – a UFO – an "unclothed female object"! We are told he saw she was "beautiful" which means this was no casual glance but rather he had a good look. While we are not always responsible for the first look, sometimes we cannot help it, we are responsible for the second look and the long hard stare.

Jesus tells us that adultery happens in the heart before the bed (Matthew 5:28), and this night a foothold was established in David's heart which would become a stronghold in his life as he planned his next move and became entwined in a web of murder and deceit. First, he sent for Bathsheba and took her to his bed. Then, after she became pregnant, he sent for her husband Uriah, one of his most loyal soldiers who was fighting on the battlefield, to come home and sleep with his wife and so cover up David's activities. When this failed and Uriah refused to sleep with his wife while his comrades were on the frontline, David planned to have him killed and sent him back with his own death warrant to give to Joab his commander. It read,

"Put Uriah out in front where the fighting is fiercest. Then withdraw from him so that he will be struck down and die."

It's almost unbelievable that David would stoop to this; but it doesn't end here. When Bathsheba had her child David took her into the palace to be his wife. Probably everyone at court would have known what happened. Months passed and David continued to rule but we read of no psalms he wrote at this time. His heart and mind were captured and tormented by other things. What began as a foothold of lust had become a stronghold of lies, deception and death. David had opened the door for demonic powers to work in his life and through him to affect the nation which he reigned over. So God sent to him a prophet called Nathan, who told him about a rich man who had many sheep, but when a visitor came to his house he stole from a neighbour an only lamb that was dearly loved and slaughtered it for a meal for his guest. When David heard this he flew into a rage and said that man *"deserves to die."*

Even when someone is in the grip of the most destructive sin and activity they can still get angry at someone else's, but they have learned to live with and become blind to their own. Nathan stares at the king and says, *"You are that man."* He tells David how God had blessed him with so much and would have given more but how he took the wife of another man and had him killed.

Spiritual footholds and strongholds have to be confronted, but most often before there is a power encounter where they are destroyed there also has to be a truth encounter where they are discerned (*it is the truth that sets us free*). And this has to be responded to with repentance and brokenness.

I have found that one of the most powerful passages of scripture for dealing with ungodly footholds and strongholds is Psalm 51. It was written by David as he poured out his soul before God, acknowledging and confessing his sin and crying out for mercy. He was a man standing on the edge of an abyss. It is the description of a man fighting for his heart and becoming broken before God.

> *Cleanse me with hyssop, and I shall be clean; wash me, and I shall be whiter than snow.*
>
> *Create in me a pure heart, O God, and renew a steadfast spirit within me.*
>
> *Do not cast me from your presence or take your Holy Spirit from me.*
>
> *Restore to me the joy of your salvation and grant me a willing spirit, to sustain me.*
>
> Psalm 51:7-12

Notice how David goes to the heart of the issue which is the issue of his own heart. He is not only asking God to cleanse him but to change him. He understands the fruit of his sin is related to the root established in his heart and mind. He is dealing with the issue of his nature not just his actions. He also pleads with God to restore his joy. Isn't it revealing how, by his illicit pleasure, he lost his joy? The pleasures of sin are for a season (Hebrews 11:25) and can be enjoyable, but they never last and there is always a price to pay. Part of that price is that you lose the power to enjoy God and the life that He gives.

David's joy was restored and so was his life. The power of sexual sin and death was demolished. There were sadly still social consequences that left their scars on his and Bathsheba's lives and David's own family, and it would have been far better if David had never fallen. The old saying that a fence at the top of a cliff is much better than an ambulance at the bottom has great wisdom and truth. Nevertheless, David got right with God and he rejoiced again in his forgiveness and salvation.

> *Praise the LORD, my soul; all my inmost being, praise his holy name. Praise the LORD, my soul, and forget not all his benefits, who forgives all your sins and heals all your diseases, who redeems your life from the pit and crowns you with love and compassion.*
>
> Psalm 103:1-4

Judas Iscariot

The name Judas was once very common, but it has now all but disappeared while on the other hand the names of Jesus' other disciples, such as Matthew, Peter and John, are always popular. No parent, it seems, wants to name their child Judas after the most infamous traitor in history.

Judas Iscariot was one of Jesus' twelve disciples. He saw most of the miracles Jesus did; the dead raised, lepers cleansed, the sight of the blind restored. He witnessed people bound by demonic powers set free and thousands fed with a few loaves and fishes. He was there when Jesus walked on the water and calmed a storm with His words. He listened to the greatest teacher who ever lived and saw how the religious leaders were unable to trick or trap Him. He was also involved in the ministry having been sent out to preach the good news of the Kingdom and heal the sick, cast out demons and raise the dead. So after being with Jesus more than three years and involved in all that happened how did he become the one who betrayed his master with a kiss?

There have been many suggestions and theories. Some say Judas had become disillusioned and angry with Jesus who he thought had become soft against the Roman occupiers; he was looking for a more military figure who would throw the Roman army out of Palestine. It is said that when Jesus entered Jerusalem on Palm Sunday and cleansed the temple instead of destroying the Roman garrison (Fort Antonia) in the city, it was for Judas the last straw. Others suggest that Judas betrayed Jesus to try and force His hand against Rome's rule.

The only insight the Gospels give us is that Judas liked money, in fact he loved it. He became the group treasurer and used to help himself to the gifts and offerings that were given to support them, (John 12:6). He had his hand in the collection, probably only a little at first as the disciples seemed to be unaware of it, but a foothold of greed would end up leading to a stronghold of betrayal for thirty pieces of silver.

Jesus was aware of what was going on and that Judas was planning to betray Him, yet He gives him every opportunity to deal with his problems. Judas, however, lives the lie and his deception grows and his greed with it.

When Mary broke her jar of expensive perfume (John 12:1-11) and poured it over Jesus' head and feet, Judas was incensed and complained of the waste saying that the oil could have been sold and the money given to the poor. It sounds reasonable at first, except we are told Judas didn't care for the poor but only himself and was angry that an opportunity was lost for siphoning off some of the money.

If we don't gain power over money, then money will seek to gain power over us; it starts with a small foothold and can end with a huge stronghold. This is the reason there are so many warnings about the love and power of money in the New Testament.

On the night Judas finally betrayed Him, Jesus told His disciples around the Passover meal that one of them would do such a thing. They all denied it, including Judas, but Jesus said that the one He gave the most choice portion of the meal to, which was the highest honour at the meal, was the person who would hand Him over to the authorities. He offered it to Judas Iscariot who hearing what was said, knowing what it meant, took it and when he did so the Bible simply and fearfully states, *"Satan entered into him,"* John 13:27. A few hours later in a garden nearby he returned with soldiers and guards to arrest Jesus and identified Him to them by a kiss.

Judas should have been there on the Day of Pentecost. He should have gone down in history as a hero of the faith. He should have been casting out demons, healing the sick and raising the dead. His name should have been with the other apostles on the foundation stones of God's city, (Revelation 21:14). Instead, he has his own infamy. He became filled with remorse, returned the thirty pieces of silver to the temple leaders and then hanged himself. The foothold that started with the love of money ended with betrayal and destruction.

Places and Nations

Ungodly footholds and strongholds not only affect people but also places and nations. The more secularised a society becomes the more sexualised it will grow as its moral framework disintegrates. It starts off being without God and quickly moves to being against God.

In the United Kingdom thirty years ago gay marriage would have been unthinkable for most people, but it has now become law. The opinion polls suggested that a majority were in favour of it, especially those under thirty. So what has happened? The swinging sixties certainly had an affect when sexual values become more liberalised and promiscuity more accepted. Society, generally, became more open to a sexually "anything goes" attitude. So we should not be so surprised that when the boundaries came down within the heterosexual community it was not going to be too long before attitudes started to shift to more acceptance of homosexual practice. After all, it's difficult to condemn sex in the homosexual community when heterosexual sexual activity is running rampant!

For instance, when I was in senior school those sexually active were considered in the minority, today, they would be in the majority. Those still virgins at 15 or 16 are, instead of being seen as virtuous, looked on as having something wrong with them.

Just look at the classification of films where a 12 or PG today seem equivalent to the X rated and 18 categories of just twenty years ago.

So, sexually what became tolerated and then accepted has today become celebrated and admired. This does not happen overnight, but when footholds are neglected strongholds become erected. Therefore, an institution such as marriage has become radically redefined and changed to allow two men or two women to be married even though the *Office for National Statistics* published in September 23, 2010, the most comprehensive breakdown on the question of how many people in Great Britain are gay. It showed that just 1.5 percent of the population consider themselves homosexual or bisexual.

So what is going to happen next?

The *Gay Liberation Front Manifesto,* published in 1971 and revised in 1978, states clearly their objectives and at the heart of them is the chilling statement "we must aim at the abolition of the family."

When we look at other nations and their sexual revolution we can see where this is heading. Denmark became the first country in the world to legalise pornography in 1969. The pornographic industry exploded there almost immediately, making Danish pornographers very wealthy and catapulting them to worldwide fame.

It established Copenhagen's infamous *Istedgade* (a street in Copenhagen) as the liberal sex capital of the world. It was also the first nation to legally recognise civil ceremony same sex partnerships in 1989. Today Denmark is also the Zoophalia, (sex with animals) capital of the world.

The first country in the world to introduce gay marriage was Holland, in 2001. The age of consent there is also one of the lowest in the world, as the country operated what was in effect an age of consent of 12, subject to qualifications such as the child's parents and the child do not object. Other societies would consider that to be paedophilia (sex with children). But Holland's so called sexual freedom doesn't end there. The politician who masterminded the gay marriage campaign in Holland says that "group marriage" is now being discussed in the country. Boris Dittrich, a former Dutch politician, gave an interview to a French gay news agency where he revealed that he softened public opinion to gay marriage by first introducing registered partnerships. He said, "We thought it might be psychologically better to first introduce registered partnerships." It was a good decision, he said, because people got used to legally recognized gay unions and called them gay marriages. The next logical step was to introduce full gay marriage by law, he said. Now he admits there are discussions about marriage for more than two people. Three-way relationships have already been recognized in Holland, under a "cohabitation agreement".

It is going to become more bizarre and frightening where this is all going to lead. Just recently the Irish Broadcasting network RTE was supporting one of its sports news presenters who identified himself as "gender fluid." Jonathan Clynch will now sometimes present the news as a man and at other times as a woman!

Whenever the will of God is rejected the devil gains a foothold, if this becomes a repeated pattern then it will become a stronghold in a person's or a nation's life.

Sow a thought, and you reap an act;
Sow an act, and you reap a habit;
Sow a habit, and you reap a character;
Sow a character, and you reap a destiny.

4

Spiritual Strongholds

A Stronghold is something
that has a " Strong hold"

Not far from where I live there are the remains of an old Roman fort that is almost 2000 years old. The Romans were great builders of fortresses and strongholds and is one of the reasons they were so successful in their conquests. Their occupation of much of England and Wales lasted for nearly 500 years. Their strategy was to first gain a foothold in a region where they would build a strong wooden stockade surrounded by ditches. Then they would strengthen and consolidate and build more substantial and powerful strongholds to control the territory they had subdued.

Shortly after 1066, following William the Conqueror's victory at the Battle of Hastings, the first castles appeared in England and Wales. The word "castle" comes from a Latin word meaning "fortress."

In the Old Testament, a stronghold was a fortified dwelling to protect its inhabitants from an enemy. The most well-known example is the city of Jerusalem which became known as the "stronghold of King David". The first time the city is mentioned is in Genesis 14 where it is referred to as "Salem" meaning "whole, safe and at peace", like the Hebrew word *Shalom*. Later, it was taken over by the Jebusites and renamed *Jebus*. They built great walls around the city and it became known for its impregnable defences and its wickedness. It sat in the midst of the Promised Land as a stronghold to Canaanite idolatry and occult practices. Its inhabitants boasted that no Israelite army would ever be able to conquer it, (2 Samuel 5:6,7). Yet David and his army captured the city and transformed it from a centre of idolatry into a stronghold of worship to God.

What is a Spiritual Stronghold?

In his book *The Three Battlegrounds*, Francis Frangipane writes,

> A demonic stronghold is any type of thinking that exalts itself above the knowledge of God, thereby giving the devil a secure place of influence in an individual's thought life. Wherever a stronghold exists it is a demonically induced pattern of thinking. Specifically, it is a house made of thoughts which has become a dwelling place for satanic activity...

These strongholds often operate as negative and destructive thought patterns which are burned into our hearts and minds by either traumatic experiences or through repetition over a long period of time. Such thinking determines our attitudes and actions and governs not just what we think but how we think.

They are revealed in un-Christ like temperaments or behaviour patterns. They develop toxic emotions and give the enemy a place to attack and influence our lives.

The aspect of human nature which has been said to be most similar to the nature of the evil one is the carnal thought life. It is uniquely in our uncrucified thoughts and unsanctified attitudes that unclean spirits influence our thinking and invade our attitudes gaining access into our lives.

A spiritual stronghold is therefore a spiritual power that not only affects our thinking and influences our emotions and decisions, but can end up controlling and ruling over them. It becomes a mind-set filled with a sense of hopelessness and helplessness that causes us to accept as unchangeable situations that are not the will of God. The presence of such a stronghold must be suspected when a Christian finds themself feeling powerless to change a situation that they already know is contrary to God's will. When someone says, "I can't forgive," when they know they should, or they are controlled by fears they know are irrational and destructive, such strongholds have usually been established.

Frangipane continues,

> If you want to identify the hidden strongholds in your life, you need only survey the attitudes in your heart. Every area in your thinking that glistens with hope in God is an area liberated by Christ. But any system of thinking that does not have hope, which feels hopeless, is a stronghold that must be pulled down.

A person without hope will always go back to their past and never move forward into their destiny. This is why the apostle

Paul says that we are to not only experience hope but to overflow with it,

> *May the God of hope fill you with all joy and peace as you trust in him, so that you may overflow with hope by the power of the Holy Spirit.*

Romans 15:13

The first promise in the Bible (Genesis 3:15) is one of hope about Jesus' first coming. And the last promise (Revelation 22:20) is the hope of Jesus' second coming. Everywhere in between the Scriptures shine with hope for the people of God.

While the root of fear is that something bad is going to happen, the root of hope is that something good is on the way. This is because God is a good God and *"Works in all things for the good of those who love Him,"* Romans 8:28. He promises that when we follow Him, *"goodness and love"* will follow us, Psalm 23:5.

One of the ways in which we activate fear is by expecting something bad to happen. This creates within us a sense of dread and foreboding which is the exact opposite of faith and hope. On the other hand, one of the ways we activate our faith is by believing something good is going to occur. This is not about the power of positive thinking which can sometimes be just silly and dangerous. Rather it is the power of godly thinking which is positive.

Everything in God's kingdom is positive. It is love, joy, peace, hope, light, life, provision, goodness and so on. While everything in the kingdom of darkness is negative. It is death, despair, disease, misery, fear, torment and everything that's bad.

The devil wants us to be negative, defeatist and pessimistic because it makes it easier for him to capture our thinking and prevent us from releasing our faith in God. He attacks our hope to undermine and destroy our faith, because *"Faith is being sure of what we hope for,"* Hebrews 11:1.

Christians must be optimists and optimistic because God is sovereign and in complete control. Pessimism makes our minds more vulnerable to satanic attack. This is why we are told to *"Put on the hope of salvation as a helmet,"* 1Thessalonians 5:8.

Habitual Sin

Ungodly thinking leads to godless actions and activity. Therefore, such strongholds in the mind reveal themselves through sinful habits and bondages. If you want to discern the spiritual powers at work in a community or city look for the most prevalent habitual sins and bondages. In some places it may have to do with drugs or sex, in others it may be violence and greed, for others it may be pride and self-righteousness or any other belief and practice that sets itself up against the knowledge of God.

In his book, *Lessons From a Father to His Son*, former USA Attorney General, John Ashcroft, recalls the day he was first sworn into the United States Senate in 1995,

> The night before, my father arranged for some close friends and family – maybe 15 to 20 people – to gather for dinner. My father eyed a piano in the corner of the room and said, "John,

why don't you play the piano and we'll sing?" "Okay dad," I said, "You name it and I'll play it." Dad said, "Let's sing, *We Are Standing On Holy Ground.*"

It was one of my father's favourites, but he was not engaging in some sentimental ploy in singing it. He had a profound purpose in his request.

The next morning the family gathered at a house not far from the Capitol that was maintained by a group of friends for the express purpose of bringing members of Congress together for spiritual enrichment. At the time Ashcroft did not realize how weak his father was. He later learned that his father had told an acquaintance of his, "I'm hanging on by a thread, and it's a thin thread at that, but I'm going to see John sworn into the Senate."

As the family gathered together, the earnestness of senior Ashcroft's voice suddenly commanded attention, "John," he said, "Please listen carefully." Everyone focused on John's dad.

"The spirit of Washington is arrogance," he said. "And the spirit of Christ is humility. Put on the Spirit of Christ. Nothing of lasting value has ever been accomplished in arrogance. Someday I hope your duties as a senator tug on your sleeve and you say, 'Senator, your spirit is showing.'"

John then knelt in front of the sofa where his father was seated, and everyone gathered closer. When John realized his father was struggling unsuccessfully to lift himself off the couch, John said, "Dad, you don't have to struggle to stand and pray over me with these friends." "John," his father answered, "I'm not struggling to stand, I am struggling to kneel."

John felt overwhelmed and inspired all at the same time. He was sworn into the Senate that afternoon. Early the next morning on January 5, 1995, a friend wakened him with the news that his father had died.

"John," the friend said, "There is something you ought to know. This was not a surprise to your dad. Yesterday, your father pulled me aside and said, 'Dick, I want you to assure me that when John gets to his assigned offices, you will have prayer with him, inviting the presence of God into those rooms.' I looked at your father and said, 'We'll do just that. And, as a matter of fact, we'll call you up in Springfield, put you on the speaker phone, and you can join us for the consecration.'

"John, the next thing I knew your father grabbed me by the arm and said, 'You don't understand. I'll be with you. But I won't be in Springfield.' He knew what was going to happen, John, he knew."

The corridors of power are often filled with the furnishings of pride, whether they be political, commercial or religious. Such pride creates a toxic building site for ungodly strongholds. The first thing we must do in such environments is make sure we guard our own hearts and minds.

In the days of the Roman Republic, the general of a particularly successful or important military campaign was occasionally awarded a "triumph". This festive ceremony featured a parade of captured bounty and prisoners, interspersed with Roman soldiers signing bawdy songs about their commander, who would wave to the cheering crowds from the back of a chariot. And behind the chariot would walk a slave, whose sole job was to whisper to the conquering hero "Remember that you are mortal."

It's worth remembering that when he was first created even the devil was good and served God in heaven. But slowly the position and power he exercised was not enough and he craved more and was cast out from the presence of God (Isaiah 14).

Why do good people become bad? Even in Christian leadership, from Popes to televangelists and from presidents to pastors, leaders have been corrupted by the power they hold. Even disciples can become like dictators and manoeuvre for position to be the greatest and have the most important position. This is why God so highly esteems humility as one of the greatest virtues (Isaiah 57:15).

It was the historian and moralist Lord Acton, writing in a letter to Bishop Mandell Creighton in 1887, who made the famous statement, *"Power tends to corrupt, and absolute power corrupts absolutely."* But he wasn't the first to voice such concerns. William Pitt the Elder, British Prime Minister from 1766 to 1778, said something similar in a speech to the House of Lords in 1770, "Unlimited power is apt to corrupt the minds of those who possess it."

To be obsessed with power is to become controlled by the power you desire.

Napoleon Bonaparte became one of the world's greatest military conquerors yet ended his days a broken man, exiled and imprisoned. He used to say,

> Power is my mistress. I have worked too hard
> at her conquest to allow anyone to take her
> away from me.

Jewish tradition tells us that King Uzziah was a cousin of the prophet Isaiah. Uzziah reigned over the kingdom of Judah for 52 years from the age of just 16, and for the majority of that time he was a great and noble leader. We are told he increased in power and prestige establishing his authority and strengthening the kingdom. There was a great list of achievements and accomplishments he had made, and the nation enjoyed peace and prosperity during which time he built a great army. Our weaknesses are often found in the shadow of our strengths and this was also Uzziah's undoing because we read that his success and adulation *made his heart proud. "But after Uzziah became powerful his pride led to his downfall,"* 2 Chronicles 26:16.

One day Uzziah decided that being king wasn't enough and he entered the Temple to burn incense on the altar. Azaraiah the priest, accompanied by 80 other priests, courageously followed and confronted the king telling him what he was doing was unlawful for only consecrated priests who were Aaron's descendants could carry out this task. They told the king he was being unfaithful to the Lord by doing this.

Uzziah had the censer of incense in his hand and was furious at being confronted. He started raging at the priests and as he was doing so leprosy started to break out over his face and body – immediately he was ushered out of the temple and that was the end of his rule. Even though Uzziah's reign lasted a little longer he did not go back to the palace but had to stay in a separate building while his sons took over the affairs of the kingdom.

He had started well but Uzziah finished badly. The whole nation became infected and corrupted,

> *From the sole of your foot to the top of your head there is no soundness—only wounds and welts and open sores, not cleansed or bandaged or soothed with oil.*
>
> Isaiah 1:6

Isaiah prophesies to this godless people knowing the king, his own cousin, had accelerated the decline and lost political, moral and spiritual oversight of the nation.

The more Uzziah ruled and prospered the more the pride of power had captured his heart and being king wasn't sufficient. He thought he could do what he wanted but ended his days clothed in fine garments which covered and concealed the rancid, rotting flesh of his own rebellion and lust for power. He reigned but lost the ability to rule long before he finally left office and died a slow tragic death.

Pride had been growing in his heart for some time and the more powerful he became the more he was consumed and corrupted by it.

It is revealing that when the Apostle Paul speaks of the devil looking for footholds (Ephesians 4), he speaks about the dangers of ungodly anger and our emotions. But when he warns about ungodly strongholds (2 Corinthians 10:3-5), he refers to mind-sets and thinking that exalts itself above God. It seems that the enemy targets the heart and our emotional being to create an entry point into our lives. Lust, fear, hurt, offence, rejection and a myriad of other heart issues are used to gain a foothold. Once these have become established they are used to build strongholds in our thinking and reasoning processes.

It was the tragic death of his young daughter that seemed to tip Charles Darwin over the edge in deciding there was no benevolent God or creator and that life was a process of natural selection.

In the Shadow of our Strengths

One of the greatest dangers of ungodly strongholds is they can often develop in the shadow of our strengths. In military strategy a stronghold is always built somewhere that is already strong, such as the top of a hill or an entrance to a bay. Satan targets our natural strengths to try and position his fortresses.

Gordon Macdonald wrote in *Restoring Your Broken World,* after he had fallen morally and was by God's grace fully restored,

> I was asked one day, "If Satan was going to try and blow you out of the water, how do you think he would do it?" I thought and all I could say was, "I really don't know, but I know one way he won't do it – that is through personal relationships." Not so long later I was committing adultery and was blown out of the water.

We are constantly aware of our weaknesses, we watch them and they can drive us to God. But our natural strengths can be a different matter. It's not just what we are bad at, but also what we are good at that can provide the foundation for footholds to be established and strongholds to become entrenched in our lives. Take for instance the response that many give to the question, "Why do you think God should forgive you?" They answer, "Because I do the best I can, I try not to do anyone any harm, I help those who are in need etc." All these things are good but can create mind-sets of self-righteousness and self-sufficiency which become great barriers in responding to the Gospel that declares, *"All have sinned and fallen short of God's glory"*. In fact, the self-righteous heart is harder to reach than the unrighteous one, because the person has to be persuaded they are lost before they can be saved. This is why Jesus had more problems with the Pharisees and religious leaders than He did the prostitutes and publicans, and why they were so hostile and hardened to the Gospel.

Experiencing God's forgiveness is realising that it is not only the bad things we have done that separate us from God but also the good things that we have relied upon (Philippians 3:1-11).

Strangleholds

The devil will use one stronghold to try and establish another and then another to build a stranglehold. His purpose isn't merely to stop us fulfilling our potential in God, he comes to steal, kill and destroy.

In the continuum of sin that the Apostle James refers to (James 1:14,15), he tells us that each person is tempted when he is lured and enticed by his own desire, desire when it has conceived gives birth to sin, sin when it is full grown brings forth death.

This is why the moment to deal with an evil thought is immediately – the instant it comes. If the devil cannot find a foothold he will never be able to build a stronghold and establish a stranglehold.

Billy Graham once said, "In any battle between the imagination and the will, the will loses every time."

What does he mean? It's simple – the battle has to be won at the very beginning in the mind, when evil thoughts first come. If we entertain those thoughts instead of rejecting them our will is already compromised and it will not be strong enough to overcome inflamed imaginations and fantasies if we allow them to take root.

Martin Luther, the great reformer, had many battles with dark spiritual powers, and observed, "You cannot stop birds from flying over your head, but you can stop them from making nests in your hair."

Sin, Lies and Deception

In his book *Passion for Jesus*, Mike Bickle has written about the way in which the devil builds these strongholds,

> First he starts with a foundation of lies and half-truths... Then up go thick walls, brick by brick; vain philosophies, erroneous interpretations of Scripture, inaccurate ideas about the person of God and distorted perceptions of how God sees and feels about you... Held together by the mortar of mistaken reasoning, the walls rise higher and higher. Soon, lofty towers of stubborn pride and vain imagination loom above the shadows.

Sin and lies are the building blocks of ungodly strongholds. Jesus called the devil *"the father of lies"* and said that when he lies he is speaking his native language, John 8:44.

The devil cannot make you sin, or in fact do anything, but he is a master of tempting us to sin and of lying and deceiving us into doing and being what he desires.

Satan gains a foothold and starts building his strongholds when we align ourselves with his lies and give place to sin within our lives.

The power of the lie is that as long as you believe it to be true, it is truth for you and it becomes your reality. When Elijah became afraid and ran for his life after the confrontation with the prophets of Baal on Mount Carmel, it was because he believed Jezebel's threats to kill him. This was never going to happen because of God's protection, however, the prophet believed the queen's lies and threats and so at that moment they became truth for him. They opened the door to the spirit behind those words and a spirit of death came against him and then upon him.

Elijah hid in the desert, sat down under a small tree and just wanted to die. Jezebel had threatened and vowed to kill herself if she did not slay Elijah – but that was just another of her lies.

Elijah needed a truth encounter. God took him to a cave in Horeb and there revealed His word and Himself to the discouraged prophet. God showed him who ruled and reigned in the nation and that Elijah was not the only righteous person left – there were thousands who had not bowed their knee to Baal and Jezebel.

Since the devil is *"the father of lies"*, John 8:44, you break his power when you expose and destroy those lies. The first piece of spiritual armour we are told to put on to withstand the devil's schemes is the *"belt of truth,"* (Ephesians 6:14). Satan's lies cannot withstand the truth any more than the darkness of night can withstand the light of the rising sun.

The devil's kingdom is built upon and operates by fear and deception. He is a deceiver and a destroyer and every title in the Bible he is given refers to these activities.

This is why throughout His earthly ministry the two things Jesus said more than any other as He confronted the kingdom of darkness were, *"I tell you the truth,"* and *"fear not."*

Footholds and Strongholds

5

Demolishing Strongholds

All Successful Deliverance Must Begin by First
Removing That Which Defends the Enemy
Francis Frangipane

The Christian writer and counsellor Selwyn Hughes gives the following insight on how he earned to discern and demolish the ungodly strongholds in people's lives;

> In the early years of my ministry, when people came to me with problems, I would frequently engage in the practice of rebuking the devil, and those prayers often brought great relief – but the mistake I made was not to sit down with people who came to me and deal with the 'beneath the surface' problems which had given Satan a foothold in their lives. By making it appear that Satan was the only problem I trivialised the issue. It's a lot easier (and less confusing) to sit down with a person and take authority over Satan than it is to think through together the tough and perplexing issues that lie beneath the surface and then work towards some biblical perspectives. But this is demanded of us if we are to help each other towards maturity.

Ungodly strongholds, by their very nature and existence, have usually been built over a passage and process of time. To destroy them we need God's wisdom and power. Here is a sevenfold strategy that I have found very effective in my own life and helping others:

Recognise

The Kingdom of darkness by its very nature conceals and hides and when we venture into it we come under its deceit and deception.

> *He who conceals his sins does not prosper, but whoever confesses and renounces them finds mercy.*
>
> Proverbs 28:3

The areas we hide in darkness are the very places of our present and future defeat. The greatest defence we can have against the devil is to maintain an honest, humble and pure heart before God.

It's amazing the ability a person has to deceive themselves, thinking that a light flirtation, a small dishonesty, a little unforgiveness and a multitude of other things can be harmless and not affect them. The Bible says it's the *"little foxes that destroy the vineyard."* This doesn't mean we live with some kind of spiritual paranoia about making small mistakes, but it does mean we must take sin and temptation seriously.

Jeb Magruder was one of President Nixon's disgraced aides in the Watergate scandal, this was his take on what went wrong, "We conned ourselves into thinking we weren't doing anything wrong and by the time we were doing things that were illegal we'd lost control."

In the book *The Heat, Steelworkers' Lives and Legends,* Joe Gutierrez tells five stories from his forty-two years as a steelworker. In one story, called *Snow Danced in August,* he describes a scene of silvery dust flakes that frequently floated to the floor in an area of the mill where steel strips rolled over pads in a tall cooling tower. For years, workers and visitors alike flocked to the sight, which was especially picturesque at night. Then they discovered the dust was asbestos. "Everybody breathed it," wrote Gutierrez, who himself suffered from the slow, choking grip of asbestosis, as did many plant workers. He comments, "Who am I? I'm everybody. Can't walk too far now. I get tired real fast and it hurts when I breathe, sometimes. And to think we used to fight over that job."

One summer, wasps built a nest in the roofing just above the back door of our house. Hundreds of them flew incessantly to and fro, swarming everywhere. It was very unpleasant and a little dangerous but the very fact they were so visible became their downfall. I simply put powdered chemicals around their nest and within a week they were dead and gone.

Symptoms of bondage and enemy activity are never pleasant but they reveal where the enemy is at work building. His activity exposes his vulnerability to the power of God for those who know how to discern it.

Prayer

Lord Jesus, open my mind and my spirit to your ways and your word. Let there be no blind spots to sin in my life. Search my heart and see that there is no wicked or offensive way within me. Lead me and guide me in your truth and enable me to walk in the light so that sin and spiritual darkness has nowhere to hide. If there are any ungodly footholds or strongholds in my life, help me to recognise them and not delude myself. Empower me through your truth and by your Spirit so that sin and the powers of sin shall have no place and no dominion in my life.

Repent

Both John the Baptist and Jesus preached, *"Repent for the Kingdom of God is at hand."* Repentance means a change of thinking and direction. Many see repentance only in a negative sense, something that deals with the mess and what's gone wrong in the past. However, this is only where it begins, because repentance also opens the door to our future and destiny allowing the life and power of God's kingdom to come in and take over.

Jesus is first described by his cousin John the Baptist as *"The Lamb of God who takes away the sin of the world"* and then, a little later, as the one who will *"baptise with the Holy Spirit and fire"*. Repentance is the way we get the sin out of our life and dealt with, and it is also the means through which we position ourselves to receive the life giving power of the Holy Spirit.

In Psalm 51 King David pours out his soul to God in one of the most public and open admissions and confessions of sin found anywhere in the Scriptures. He had not come to this place easily, but when brought face to face with his sin and crimes by the words of the prophet Nathan, David accepted what he had done and what he had become. He comes broken before the Lord with cries of deep repentance. It was the place where his forgiveness and freedom had to begin.

I will never forget the time my wife and I were ministering to a dear lady whose life had been ravaged by physical and mental sickness. She had come to faith in Christ and truly loved God, but there was still so much healing and freedom she needed. It became obvious though ministering to her there were a lot of demonic powers that had a hold on her. Initially, many of these forces were quickly broken and dealt with as we prayed with her, but we had now hit a wall. We suggested she find a quiet place in the church, which was empty except for myself, my wife and some of our ministry team, and that she read through Psalm 51. We left her but watched carefully. Several minutes later we saw and heard her sobbing almost uncontrollably. We waited before we rushed in and eventually the weeping stopped and she had great peace. We asked her what had happened and were told that as she read the Psalm something broke within her and she felt freedom and cleansing flowing. She said that when she became a Christian it was because she realised how much she needed God. This day, however, she came face to face with the consequences of her sin and felted broken because of what she had done and been and also with how much Jesus loved her and was able to cleanse and heal her. When we prayed with her following this experience, demonic blockages and powers were broken and dealt with easily.

In his book *Word and Spirit,* RT Kendall makes a very perceptive statement about spirituality when he says, "I sometimes define spirituality as closing the time gap between sin and repentance. In other words, how long does it take to admit I was wrong?"

Prayer

Lord Jesus, I thank you for the power of your blood that not only forgives but is able to cleanse me from all unrighteousness and the power and pollution of sin. I acknowledge my sin and selfish ways, and accept and receive your grace. I will not live under condemnation because your word says there is no condemnation for those who are in Christ Jesus, (Romans 8:1). And I will not live with guilt or accusation because you have promised that when we confess our sins you will remember them no more. I declare today that through repentance and the power of your blood I am forgiven and my sins have been washed away.

Renounce and Rebuke

> *Submit yourselves, then, to God. Resist the devil, and he will flee from you.*
>
> James 4:7

The great Dutch evangelist Corrie ten Boom, often spoke about the importance of what she called *"closing the circle"* against the enemy. She says,

> It would seem that after having been a Christian for almost eighty years that I would no longer do ugly things that need forgiving. Yet I am constantly doing things to others that cause me to have to go back and ask for their forgiveness. Sometimes these things I actually do – other times they are simply attitudes I let creep in which break the circle of God's perfect love.
>
> I first learned the secret of "closing the circle" from my nephew, Peter van Woerden, who was spending the weekend with me in our apartment in Baarn, Holland. He asked me if I remembered a person that we had prayed for called Jan. He was a young man we had prayed

for many times. He had a horrible demon of darkness in his life and although we fasted and prayed and cast it out in the Name of Jesus, the darkness always returned.

Peter shared that he had learned a great lesson from what happened with Jan. He said that God showed him that if a Christian walks in the light then the blood of Jesus cleanses him from all sin making his life a closed circle and protecting him from all outside dark powers. But if there is unconfessed sin in his life, the circle has an opening – a gap – and this allows the dark powers to come back in. "But when I led Jan to confess his unconfessed sin the circle was closed and the dark powers could no longer return."

Corrie says that the more she thought about this she realised that Peter had learned a truth from the Lord. The devil is a legalist. This means that if he has any right to affect and afflict our lives he will use it and will not relinquish it until it is taken away.

On the cross Jesus won a total, complete, irrevocable victory over Satan and every demonic force. Through renouncing sin and rebuking Satan we are not seeking to win victory but rather applying the victory that Jesus has already won.

We need to speak to those sins that have tainted us and the powers behind them that taunt us and take authority over them in Jesus' name. To do this effectively we must know and exercise our spiritual authority and who we are in Christ and who He is in us. Simply saying words or reciting prayers is never enough, they must be empowered by God's truth and His

Spirit. Whereas repentance is directed towards God, renouncing involves one's own soul and rebuking is aimed at the devil.

Prayer

Jesus Christ, I confess and I proclaim that you are the Lord of my life and that your shed blood for me at the cross of Calvary has established you my Redeemer. This moment, I rededicate my life to you that you can have complete rule over my life. In the name of Jesus Christ I submit every dark and sinful thought and desire I have entertained into your nail pierced hands. I renounce Satan and all his works and I rebuke every power and agent of sin and the enemy from my life. By the authority given me in Luke 10:19, I take authority over every spirit that has set itself up over the sins of my life and I command them and rebuke them (name them individually) to leave me forever.

Receive

In Psalm 103 we see how David had received God's forgiveness and cleansing which he prayed for in Psalm 51,

> *Praise the Lord, O my soul; all my inmost being, praise his holy name. Praise the Lord, O my soul, and forget not all his benefits – who forgives all your sins and heals all your diseases, who redeems your life from the pit and crowns you with love and compassion.*
>
> *For as high as the heavens are above the earth, so great is his love for those who fear*

him; as far as the east is from the west, so far has he removed our transgressions from us.

Psalm 103:1-4,11-12

We receive by faith and thanksgiving.

Prayer

Lord Jesus, I come to you with a thankful heart for all you have done and are doing in my life. Your mercies are new to me every morning and great is your faithfulness. I thank you for my salvation. I thank you for healing, cleansing and deliverance and freedom through your shed blood and resurrected life. I thank you that the same Spirit that raised you from the dead lives in me and gives life to my mortal body. Thank you that you have promised never to leave me or forsake me and that you are able to keep me from falling and to present me before his glorious presence without fault and with great joy (Jude 24).

Rejoicing

My wife and I were asked to visit a young lady in her early thirties who had become a very sad alcoholic. She had been a Christian since her teens but due to a moral failure that she was enticed into by a pastor much older than her, she found herself with three young children, fathered by this now former pastor, and living a desperately sad life. She badly wanted to break free from the bondage and brokenness she found herself in. We counselled and prayed with her and led her through the steps of repentance I have mentioned. This began the process of healing and wholeness she longed for. At the end of the prayer time her face was beaming with peace and hope, tears of joy were running down her cheeks and she was filled with thanksgiving for what God was doing in her life. We encouraged her to rejoice and be thankful and I said to her that while I have no power to forgive sin, only God can do that, she needed to know that if she sincerely called upon God for forgiveness she was forgiven and I spoke the words over her life "you are forgiven". Because of the situation she had found herself in, taken advantage of, abused and broken, those words were the start of a road to healing for herself and her children.

Liberation calls for celebration. Jesus said there is rejoicing in heaven over every sinner who repents.

Prayer

Heavenly Father, I thank you that you are the God who saves, heals and delivers. I thank you that your word says that when one sinner repents there is rejoicing in heaven. I thank you that this joy of forgiveness and freedom is now also in my heart and even though I do not rely on feelings and emotions, but your word and your truth, I lift up my voice to rejoice for all that you have done and are doing in my life.

Respond

The purpose of God's Kingdom coming into our lives is not only about forgiveness and freedom but regime change. It is a change of government. It's about establishing God's rule and reign in every area of our lives.

Prayer

Lord God, I honour you as King over every area and in every part of my life. I desire your ways to direct and guide me. I know that your Word brings not only information but transformation and I ask for your help to respond to what it says in ways that please you. Thank you for the truth that not only sets me free but also keeps me free.

Footholds and Strongholds

6

The Stronghold of Offence

No matter how long you nurse a grudge,
it won't get better.

A brother wronged is more unyielding
than a fortified city; disputes are like the
barred gates of a citadel.
Proverbs 18:9

Could a slap on the face have caused the greatest massacre of Russian troops in a single conflict in the history of warfare? Could the intense rivalry and hatred between two Russian generals be the reason why over 250,000 of their own soldiers were captured, injured or killed during just one battle?

Erik Durschmied, in his book *How Chance And Stupidity Altered The Course Of Military History* says that was exactly what took place. Defeat at the Battle of Tannenberg fought against the German army in the first month of World War 1 (August 26-30, 1914) resulted in the almost complete destruction of the Russian Second Army, and the suicide of its commanding general, Alexander Samsonov.

Durschmied, along with other military historians, has suggested that the outcome of the battle could well have been determined ten years earlier. While exact details have been disputed there is no doubt that the two Russian generals who lead the Tsar's First and Second Armies, Pavel Rennenkampf and Alexander Samsonov, disliked each other intensely. The reason for much of their mutual dislike stems from what happened between them during the Russo-Japanese war of 1904-5. They were then both divisional commanders, equal in rank, when Samsonov's Siberian Cossack Division was ordered to defend the Tentai Coal Mines in Manchuria while Rennenkampf's division held the adjoining sector and received specific orders to support Samsonov's Cossacks. The Japanese attacked Samsonov whose division was routed with heavy loss of life while Rennenkampf stood by and did nothing.

A few days after this bloody disaster, it was reported the two generals met by chance on the railway platform at Mukden Station and an infuriated Samsonov rushed to Rennenkampf took off his gloves and slapped his rival across the face. A bitter argument ensued and their hatred for each other and desire for revenge remained. This fact was overlooked when they were later appointed to lead Russia's two adjoining armies. One man who didn't forget the incident that day was a foreign military observer, a German captain Max Hoffman.

At Tannenberg the Russian armies advanced too hastily; Samsonov had been ordered to join up with Rennenkampf but he couldn't because his army was in a mess, ill equipped, ill prepared and transportation and communications were a nightmare. Yet despite this because of massive numerical advantage the Russians broke through German lines on several fronts and Russian High Command became convinced they had won the battle.

Max Hoffman, who was now a Colonel at German High Command, devised a master plan to strike at the Russian army and win the conflict. It was for a concentration of German forces to be thrown against Samsonov while leaving only a thin cavalry screen to deceive Rennenkampf. But the German High Command were worried about Rennenkampf moving his 300,000 men southwards with only two German cavalry divisions between them and the destruction of the German Eighth army. It was at this moment Colonel Hoffman reassured General Hindenberg and told him of the incident at the railway station and the Russian generals' hatred for each other. Hindenberg took his advice and by the time the battled ended on August 30, Samsonov's Second Army was destroyed. Max Hoffman had been right, Rennenkampf had refused to do anything to help.

What is Offence?

Apart from personal sin nothing will destroy your ministry, peace and joy faster and more destructively than the spirit and stronghold of offence.

The word "offence" comes from the Greek word *skandalon,* which means a snare, a noose or a trap. It was the name of the part of the trap on which bait was hung to lure its victims. Satan uses offences as bait to lure us into a life-time of hatred, bitterness, resentment and unforgiveness. The word also came to mean a stumbling block so that when we allow the spirit of offence to come into our lives, it becomes a hindrance and an obstacle to us. It causes us to stumble in our walk with God and our journey through life. We also get the word "scandal" and "scandalised" from it, which means to be outraged, shocked and horrified. So generally it means to feel annoyed or hurt by something or what someone did or said.

In warfare there are a variety of weapons the enemy uses and one of the devil's most powerful is the spirit of offence. It has caused more pain and divisions in our world and the church than almost anything else.

Jesus spoke a great deal about offences and their power. He said, *"If your right eye causes you to stumble (skandalon) gouge it out and throw it away,"* Matthew 5:29. He is not saying we are to self mutilate ourselves but rather to take sin and offences seriously otherwise they will end up destroying us and anyone else they capture.

He said to His disciples, *"Things that cause people to stumble (skandalon) are bound to come, but woe to anyone through whom they come,"* Luke 17:1. Because of sin our world is full of offences and we are warned to make sure they do not come through us or become a part of our lives.

The best selling author and motivational speaker Dale Carnegie recounts a trip to Yellowstone Park in Wyoming, America, and a visit to the place where the grizzly bears are fed. He did not have to wait long before one came into the clearing where food had been placed to entice him. The guide told the people that the grizzly could whip any animal in the West with the possible exceptions of the buffalo and the Kodiak bear. As they watched, the tourists noticed that there was only one other animal that the grizzly would allow to eat with him and take some of his food – a skunk. They were told, of course, that the bear could whip that old skunk and he resented him taking his food and was maddened by the skunk's brazen impudence. But he didn't strike out at it. Why?

Because, said the guide, that old grizzly was far smarter than most people, he knew there would be a high cost in trying to get even.

The Power of Offence

Offence is not a little problem. It opens the door to the demonic and can become a stronghold in our lives. Its power affects both the heart (emotions) and the mind (intellect) which are the gateway to our spirit. When we cause or take offence we can open the door for a sprit of death, hatred, murder, jealousy, anger, bitterness and resentment. I know these are strong words but let me prove it to you.

Cain and Abel

This is the first physical death and murder we read of in the Bible and human history. Cain's resentment and jealousy of his brother's sacrifice accepted by God while his own offering was rejected opened the door to a spirit of murder within his heart. We are told Cain took offence, *"So Cain was very angry, and his face was downcast,"* Genesis 4:5. The Hebrew word is *charah* which means to be incensed and burn with indignation and wrath; and what was in Cain's heart showed on his face.

This is something I have noticed many times with offended people – what they carry in their heart they also wear on their face. They look indignant, miserable and depressed. The saying "if looks could kill" aptly applies to them. It reminds me of a minister who discovered at the last minute that he hadn't invited an elderly member to attend the church picnic. He called around at her house and she opened the door and glared angrily at him. He apologised and offered to take her in his car but she refused. He apologised and encouraged her to accept but she snapped at him, "It's too late! I've already prayed for rain!"

In one of the churches I pastored someone came to see me one day with a list of what he claimed was everything wrong within the church. He came not with a compassionate attitude but with a critical analysis. I listen patiently and then I told him that my list of things that could be done better was longer than his. What I also wanted to say but didn't was that he was towards the top of that list. He had just returned from a musicians and worship conference and began to explain the imperfections of our praise and worship and started to draw me diagrams of how it should be done. I couldn't help but smile because his wife was the pianist who helped lead the worship. I also challenged him as to why he rarely sang or showed much response during the singing. He told me that when we got it right he would do so. I shared with him that true worship was first about the "heart" and not the "art". He took offence and shortly after left the church.

God warned Cain, *"Why are you angry? And why has your countenance fallen? If you do well, will not your countenance be lifted up? And if you do not do well, sin is crouching at the door; and its desire is for you, but you must master it."* We cannot stop ourselves being hurt or upset but we can make sure it doesn't take root in our heart. If we do not master "offences" they will master us.

Part of Cain's judgement for killing his brother was to become a wanderer for the rest of his life. I have noticed with those who live in offence that they are always restless, searching but never finding, moving from church to church and relationship to relationship but never content.

Jesus and the Religious and Political Leaders

Jesus did His first miracle at a wedding turning water into wine, John 2:1-11. After that He travelled to Jerusalem and went into the Temple and drove the money changers and animal sellers out of its forecourts, John 2:14-16. They were extorting the pilgrims coming to Passover with inflated prices and corrupt practices. He caused quite a stir. Have you ever stopped to ponder how amazing this is? Jesus begins His mission with a sign and wonder at a wedding celebration and then He goes to the most religious place on the face of the earth and drives everyone out. A religious mindset would have it the other way around with Jesus doing miracles in the Temple and reproving the wedding guests for drinking too much wine. But Jesus is more at home and His glory revealed at a party where He is honoured and welcomed than in a religious place where He is not.

This was only the start of Jesus upsetting the religious and political leaders who lorded it over the common people. The Pharisees and the Sadducees, who loved their religious power, along with the Romans and the Herodians, who loved their political and worldly power, all opposed the ministry of Jesus and His Church. When He offended the Pharisees by healing on the Sabbath they planned and schemed to kill Him, (Matthew 12:14, 15:12).

John the Baptist and the Queen of Galilee

The power and significance of the first few verses of Luke chapter three are not immediately obvious until you ponder them,

In the fifteenth year of the reign of Tiberius Caesar—when Pontius Pilate was governor of Judea, Herod tetrarch of Galilee, his brother Philip tetrarch of Iturea and Traconitis, and Lysanias tetrarch of Abilene, during the high priesthood of Annas and Caiaphas, the word of God came to John son of Zechariah in the desert.

Luke 3:1,2

God bypassed all the "great and the powerful" in the religious and political world of the day and came to a man called John and known as "John the Baptist" who was living in the wilderness. So began one of the most powerful prophetic ministries calling a nation back to God and preparing the way for the coming of the Messiah.

John, however, became hated by some of those whose sin he reproved and one such woman was Herodias, the Queen of Galilee. She was rebuked by John for her marriage to Herod Antipas after she had already been married to and then divorced from his brother. She took great offence at what John was saying about her and plotted his death, *"For John had been saying to Herod, 'It is not lawful for you to have your brother's wife.' So Herodias nursed a grudge against John and wanted to kill him,"* Mark 6:18,19.

When her daughter, Salome, danced and pleased the king so much he promised to give her anything she asked for, she conspired with her mother and requested John's head on a platter.

Jesus at Nazareth

Northern Israel was very different to the south of the country. It was mainly made up of those who worked the land and sea. They were ordinary, everyday people, simple in their ways and lifestyle. It is said of them, *"The common people heard Him gladly,"* Mark 12:37. Jesus often spoke to them in stories and parables about everyday life.

One of the major reasons why John's Gospel is so different from Matthew, Mark and Luke is because of the different location. John's Gospel is set mainly in the south where the great religious centres of Jericho and Jerusalem were. It was here that Jesus faced His most fierce opposition and where He was crucified. This is why it has no parables or stories but is filled with long theological arguments and debates as Jesus confronted the religious establishment and they plotted His execution.

It also explains why on Palm Sunday the crowds cried out "Hosanna" and laid palm branches for Jesus' triumphal entry into Jerusalem but just five days later the crowd cried, *"Crucify Him! We have no king but Caesar."* They were different groups of people. It was those from the north who had travelled to Jerusalem for the Passover who praised Jesus and they were camped outside the city unaware of the religious leaders having Jesus tried at night (breaking their own law) and then again very early in the morning. They wanted the matter settled before the northerners realised what had taken place.

There was one place in the north, however, where Jesus was attacked and rejected, and it was in His home town of Nazareth. It was here that He said, *"A prophet is not without honour except in his own town and in his own home,"* Matthew 13:27. The reason Jesus said this is because, *"they took offence at him."* The people were filled with anger and resentment and so Jesus did not do many miracles there because of their lack of faith.

This wasn't the only time Jesus was rejected at Nazareth, on a previous occasion the people had tried to kill Him. We read in Luke 4 that Jesus was at first welcomed in the local synagogue and invited to preach on the Sabbath. This was not Jesus' first sermon as is often preached, in fact He had already been ministering for about a year (His early Judean ministry is recorded only in John 1-5) and had caused quite a stir with His teachings and miracles. This is why He was invited to speak. Those from Nazareth were in a state of awe and bewilderment. They were amazed at what they were hearing as this local lad who had grown up in the town fixing furniture was now fixing bodies and changing lives.

Jesus read from Isaiah the Prophet (Isaiah 61:1-3) concerning the reason God had sent Him and everyone present was *"amazed at His gracious words"*. They loved Him and what He was saying and doing but then it all turned ugly and moments later they drove Him outside the synagogue to the edge of the town to try and throw Him over a cliff and murder Him. Jesus survived several assassination attempts like this because His purpose and time had not yet come. He was not ready to die.

But why did the people change so quickly? One moment praising Him and then trying to kill Him?

It was because Jesus exposed their religious prejudice and their nationalistic pride. He says that the grace of God came to Namaan, a Syrian, and a widow in Zarephath, a Sidonian, and not to the lepers and widows in Israel. He was saying that the way to experience the love and power of God was not by relying on their religion or nationalism but in humbling themselves before God.

The only way a person can come to God is either as a sinner to a saviour or a child to a Father. No one can come as a professor or doctor, a king or a queen, a president or CEO. Our religious, professional and worldly titles do not impress God. How could they? He is Almighty and created everything. The only thing we are told impresses Him is a *"humble and contrite heart and spirit,"* Isaiah 57:14.

Jesus offended the people's minds revealing what was in their hearts and they exploded with anger. Instead of responding in humility they rose up in hostility to kill Him.

That day could have been the greatest in that town's history with multitudes saved, healed and delivered instead, it became one of its saddest and most notorious moments.

Would You Oppose a Move of God?

Think carefully before you answer that question. Sadly, every powerful move of God in history has had its opponents as well as its proponents, and regrettably many of those who have stood against God moving have come from inside the church. What is so distressing is that some of them were good men and women who had been praying for God's outpouring for years. I am reminded of the great Bible expositor G. Campbell Morgan who said about revival, "I want to be God's next new thing." He was so moved by the Welsh Revival of 1904/5 that he wrote a pamphlet entitled *Revival in Wales*. This God used in preparing the way for what took place in the Pentecostal outpouring at Azusa Street just a few years later, as thousands of these tracts were distributed among the churches in Los Angeles. Tragically, when the Pentecostal Revival came he opposed it. He described it as a work of the devil and called it, "the last vomit of Satan before Christ's return." Today the Pentecostal movement is the fastest growing in the world.

John Wesley took to preaching in the open air not because he loved the great outdoors but because pulpit after pulpit became closed to him as he preached the necessity of the New Birth. After the Methodists came the Salvation Army and William Booth and they were criticised by many from within Methodism. Tragically, those who come out of the last move of God are often the first to criticize the next.

Francis Frangipane says, "Satan's deception during a Move of God is both subtle and powerful because the devil's guise is a religious spirit. He cloaks his activity by honouring what God has done, while fighting what God is doing."

The two greatest hindrances to a Move of God's Spirit in renewal and revival are the spirit of offence and a lack of discernment.

Jesus warned that in the last days before His coming again one of the signs would be that His followers would be persecuted and many would be "offended" (*skandalisthēsontai*) and betray and hate one another. At the same time many false prophets would arise and deceive many, Matthew 24:10,11. When people are offended they are more easily deceived. This is true both of believers and unbelievers. Church history has shown that many a good and godly person or spiritual leader has condemned a genuine work of God because there were aspects of it they did not like, confusing their personal preference and likes and dislikes for true spiritual discernment.

The Jews, who longed for their Messiah, rejected Jesus because He did not fit into their preconceived ideas and theology of how He should act and what He should say. The cross, instead of being the place of wonder, became an obstacle of offence. The Apostle Paul describes it like this, *"We preach Christ crucified: a stumbling block (skandalon) to Jews and foolishness to Gentiles,"* 1 Corinthians 1:23. They were so offended by the possibility of a crucified Messiah that a veil covered their minds (2 Corinthians 3:13-16) and allowed Satan, the god of this world, to blind them to the truth, (2 Corinthians 4:4).

Do Not Be Offended

> *Great peace have they who love Your law; nothing shall offend them or make them stumble.*

> Psalm 119:165

Jesus was once asked which was the greatest of all God's commandments and He replied by saying it was to love God with all we are and have and to love others. When we love God's laws we love Him and others as we should and this stronghold of love protects us from every offence that comes against us.

We have to develop a Kingdom mindset because often differences in culture or background create and cause offences. What is perfectly acceptable in our own custom may be deeply offensive to another tradition. In my own Welsh culture when someone gives us a gift we often open it straight away and may even ask where they got it from! In other cultures to do that would be considered very bad manners. But while we need to be sensitive to our traditions as Christians we must "bow" all our nationalistic and societal cultures to a Kingdom culture of refusing to take offence especially when the other person is unaware that one has been given.

We have to make up our mind and choose not to become offended. There are many things that can cause us to become so but we do not have to take them into our heart. Here is just a short list of ways offences can come:

i)   Rejection

ii)   Not being included or invited to an event

iii)   Not getting your own way

iv)   People who do not like us

v)   People who ignore our opinion

vi)   Being made to wait

vii)   Not being treated how we think we deserve

viii)   Not being helped by those we have helped

ix)   Not being consulted

x)   Being gossiped about…

The list can be endless but we must be determined not to take offence and refuse it every time it is offered. Otherwise it will destroy our peace, rob our joy, lose us friends, divide our church, ruin our life and destroy our ministry. We cannot walk in love and live in offence. Neither do we always have to ignore what's wrong, we can point those things out but we must not harbour them. If we want to be like Jesus we must be willing to give up the right to react like other people. We cannot live and minister effectively without love and we cannot love when we carry offence in our hearts. This is why the apostle writes,

> *And this I pray, that your love may abound still more and more in knowledge and all discernment, that you may approve the things that are excellent, that you may be sincere and without **offence** till the day of Christ.*

> Philippians 1:9,10

The devil launches aggressive attacks against us to make us and keep us offended because he knows how powerful and destructive this is. Paul had many occasions when he could have been offended but he refused them all. At his first trial no one stood with him (2 Timothy 4:6) but he refused to be offended. Only one church helped him financially when he was in great need (Philippians 4:10), again he refused to become offended. Jesus also had numerous occasions to be offended but choose not to be. His own relatives were ashamed of Him, His disciples deserted Him, Peter denied Him, the religious leaders constantly tried to trap Him but He refused to take offence. He was secure in who He was and people secure in God are more free to be concerned about what people are doing to themselves than what they are doing to them.

Reconciliation is the Answer

We must learn to have closures on our offences and pull down any strongholds that have been erected in our hearts.

But what do you do if you have offended someone? Jesus said we are to go to that person and seek to be reconciled. This does not mean that you have to agree with them or give in to them but be willing to agree to disagree and move forward. You may never be the best of friends but you must not remain enemies.

What if someone has offended you? Then you follow what Jesus taught in Matthew 18:15-17, first go privately and tell them what they did. If they will not listen take one or two others along with you and go to them again. If they still refuse to listen then involve the church and if they refuse to listen even to the church then treat them as you would an unbeliever because that is the way they are acting. The goal, however, is not confrontation but reconciliation. You must not go to show them how bad they are but how good God is. Therefore, do not go until you have forgiven the person from your heart and to love them is to want what is best for them.

One of the reasons offended people are so unyielding is because it is very difficult to try and reason with them as offences are usually deeply emotional issues. Offence affects us at an emotional level – we feel hurt. There was no doubt an aspect of this among those in Nazareth, (Luke 4:16-30). The town is not even mentioned in the Old Testament and it was a small inconsequential village nestling in a hollow in the hills south of Galilee. There was also great rivalry between different towns and the people of Nazareth would have been all too aware of comments like Nathanael in John 1:46, *"Can anything good come out of Nazareth?"* Such sensitivity and rejection are often the crucible where offences are gathered.

The devil loves to attack unresolved emotional issues in our lives and one of the biggest of these is rejection. Rejection usually works in a cycle; you have been rejected – you feel like a reject – you fear more rejection – you reject others before they have a chance to reject you. It is a miserable place to live and people often take offence not because what was said or done was something terrible but because it stirred other unsettled and damaged emotions and memories.

Every unhealed wound is a target for the enemy and can become a trigger that causes you to respond in anger and pain whenever it is brought up.

When I was a young Christian, the power of offence took me captive and drove me from the church I was attending. About 30 of us from the fellowship went on a week-long mission to a seaside resort in the south of England. I had been so excited and looking forward to it and was keen to be involved. When we arrived at the church which was accommodating us, the women slept upstairs and the men were to sleep in the basement. To make it a little more comfortable the church had taken rubber mats for the men to lay on the cold basement floor beneath the sleeping bags and airbeds. While the mats were being given out I was upstairs helping someone and when I went down below I discovered all the mats were gone and I was the only one without. Not only that, one of the leaders, seeing a mat left over, had taken two. Instead of going to him and explaining, memories and emotions of past rejections surfaced and I took offence. The next week became one of the most miserable of my life. I was simmering with hurt and anger and nursing my wrath. When the pastor asked me to share my testimony or do anything I angrily responded I wouldn't. Before I went on the mission I had bought a new reference Bible but I was too upset to read it and actually tried to sell it to others on the team! When they asked me why I wanted to sell it and why I was so miserable I wouldn't tell them. To be honest I was angry, upset and hurt and felt a bit stupid telling them the reason I was so miserable and wanted to get rid of my new Bible was because I didn't have a rubber mat!

Looking back many years later, I see clearly now how the devil used what happened not only to attack me but also the whole mission. I must have been a right pain in the neck for the pastors and leaders. I carried with me an atmosphere of misery and heaviness. When the end of the week came I couldn't wait to get back home and decided to stop going to church. I would even drive past the church during service times as people were going in so they could see me "not going".

After several weeks of misery I had had enough and decided I needed to meet the pastor and apologise for my behaviour. I never told him it was about "a mat," it seemed so stupid because while that had initially been the issue the real problem was within my heart. But isn't this so often the case with offences? We find it hard to talk about what caused them because they seem so insignificant, but what they do is ignite deep unresolved issues in our hearts. It's like the person in church who is asked to help serve tea and coffee or help in the car park and bluntly refuses. When you probe why, they say, "Three years ago I served someone a cup of tea after the meeting and they didn't say 'thank you,'" or "I once helped in the church car park but someone got upset with me." I understand what they are saying but what it means is that, Jesus loved them so much He shed His blood and gave His life for them, and yet now they refuse to help or serve in church because someone was upset and didn't say "thank you".

The deception of offences is that once you start to gather them they blind you to your own character faults and failings because you only see what's wrong with others and not with yourself. It's what Jesus was referring to when He said,

> *"Why do you look at the speck of sawdust in your brother's eye and pay no attention to the plank in your own eye?*
>
> *"How can you say to your brother, 'Let me take the speck out of your eye,' when all the time there is a plank in your own eye? You hypocrite, first take the plank out of your own eye, and then you will see clearly to remove the speck from your brother's eye."*

Matthew 7:3-5

That night in his office, the pastor graciously and lovingly told me, "David, this experience will either leave you bitter or better, you have to choose." I said, "Pastor, I am so sorry, I want it to leave me better." Six months later I felt God's call to go to Bible College, 34 years later, I am sitting here writing this, I have pastored several churches, written some twenty books and travelled and ministered in over a dozen nations and it may all never have happened because of a silly rubber mat. Isn't that just stupid? But I know of two brothers who didn't speak to each other for over 25 years because they had an argument at a football match. How tragic. Life is too short and

Jesus is too wonderful to let offences and unforgiveness steal our lives.

Yet, there are times when the scars are so painful and the wounds so deep that it is hard to forgive. When you have been hurt deeply or someone you love has been damaged by the pain of abuse or betrayal then forgiveness can be the hardest thing to do. But if we don't forgive we die inside and life becomes even more unbearable.

Forgiveness is a decision and not just an emotion. The feelings come later but first it is an act of the will. When you choose to forgive you are not giving permission for the same thing to be done again. Neither are you saying that what happened doesn't matter. It does matter and those who did it must answer to God, they do not simply get away with anything. Forgiveness is putting what has happened into God's hands and letting Him deal with it.

The Greek word for forgiveness is *alpheimi* and means *to send away*. If someone dumped rubbish in your home you wouldn't let it stay there and rot. So if someone dumps rubbish in your heart why leave it decay and go toxic? If you don't want it in your home then why should you leave it fester in your heart?

One of the biggest hindrances to releasing forgiveness is the pain of "It's not fair!" Or a wounding that cries, "It's not fair what they did, it's not fair what happened!" But God offers us something much greater than fairness, He gives us grace. It is not fair that Jesus took the punishment for our sins but it is amazing grace. If we are willing at such times to lay down our demand for fairness, God's grace will not only heal and set us free but release grace into the situation to empower to restore and reconcile.

7

Building Godly Strongholds

The Lord is my rock, my fortress and my
deliverer; my God is my rock, in whom I
take refuge. He is my shield and the horn of
my salvation, my stronghold.

Psalm 18:2

Several months after I became a Christian I felt like giving up. It wasn't that I didn't want to follow Jesus, it was because I wanted to follow Him so much, however, there was one besetting sin that kept biting and binding me. One evening, I knelt at my bedside to pray with tears streaming down my face. I felt demoralized and defeated. Why was this one thing so hard to deal with? I cried to God to help me and began to read my Bible, asking Him to lead me to a scripture that would speak directly into my specific need. I turned the pages and read,

How can a young man keep his way pure?
By living according to your word. I seek you
with all my heart; do not let me stray for
your commands. I have hidden your word in
my heart that I might not sin against you.

Psalm 119:9-11

91

I had never seen those words before in the Bible and they leapt from the page bringing healing and hope. I began to understand the difference between God's conviction over sin and the devil's condemnation because of it. The devil comes and condemns, scornfully mocking and saying that we might as well give up and we will never be any use. The Holy Spirit, however, comes to convict and helps us to repent and change because God loves us and desires to heal and restore. Condemnation creates hopelessness while conviction always carries hope. I also began to understand that it wasn't enough to hate sin, we also have to love righteousness and to *"put off the old and put on the new,"* Ephesians 4:22-24.

There were strongholds of sinful mind-sets and desires that needed to be pulled down in my life but, even more, there were godly strongholds of righteous attitudes and desires that needed to be established in their place.

I was trying so hard to change myself but the answer was to cooperate with the Holy Spirit and allow Him to change me and establish His rule in my life.

The best way to deal with ungodly attitudes and passions is to turn from them and put godly ones in their place. We are not called to focus on ourselves, the battle or the devil, except when they hinder our transformation into Christ's likeness. Our calling is to focus on Jesus and be transformed into His likeness.

That night at my bedside, the tears changed from ones of defeat to those of hope and victory. The way for a *"young man"* to live pure was to seek after God with all his heart and allow His word to establish mighty fortresses of truth and righteousness within his heart. The way to deal with ungodly strongholds is to pull them down and build godly ones in their place.

Replacing Ungodly Strongholds with Godly Ones

Mark Twain once said he spent a lot of money tracing his family tree, then twice as much trying to keep it a secret!

This reminds me of the American family that wanted its history written, so they hired a professional biographer. However, they were worried about Uncle George, the black sheep of the family, who had been executed in the electric chair for murder. "No problem," said the biographer. "I will say that Uncle George occupied a Chair of Applied Electronics at an important government institution. He was attached to his position by the strongest of ties, and his death came as a real shock."

When it comes to your family's past you cannot do much except learn from it; but you can make sure it doesn't ruin and control your future. It's not our history but our destiny that God is most concerned about. Gideon grew up in a family of idol worshippers. One night God told him, *"...Tear down your father's altar...Then build a proper kind of altar to the Lord..."* Judges 6:25-26.

Gideon knew this was a moment that would change his life and family forever. Baal was a powerful demonic idol worshipped for provision and prosperity. What is so ironic is that like all idols it wasn't much help because the people were impoverished by their enemies yet still they clung onto their false gods. When Gideon destroyed Baal's shrine the town's people wanted to stone him. However, he not only demolished the ungodly altar but built a godly one in its place. There is no neutrality in the realm of the Spirit.

Long before King David made Jerusalem his capital, the city was occupied by the Jebusites and the city stronghold was known as *Jebus*.

The Jebusites were one of the Canaanite tribes that polluted the land by their idolatry and evil. They were a powerful warring nation whose name means "to tread down". They were so confident of their prowess that they boasted to David that their weakest warriors could defeat him and he would never be able to capture their stronghold (2 Samuel 5:6-10). This city stood in the midst of the Promised Land and had never been taken. Not only was its presence mocking God's people – it was intimidating and dominating.

The city defences were heavily fortified and David needed all his skill and God's guidance to defeat it. His men gained access through a water system and captured the city. In 1867 the British explorer Charles Warren, while excavating in the city, discovered a 40-foot vertical opening through solid rock, which came to be called Warren's Shaft. The channel was near a system of tunnels around the Gihon Spring, Jerusalem's only natural source of water located outside the city walls to the south. The tunnels must have provided access to the spring when the city was under siege and also provided David's warriors their point of entry.

David renamed the city *Jerusalem* meaning the City of Peace – quite a transformation from the city of war and aggression against God's people.

The Jebusites ridiculed David and his army saying, "This stronghold will never fall". It's the same mocking voice that is heard when the devil says "you will never be free" "this addiction can never be broken" "these things have been in your life for too long." But David knew that with God with him and for him, nothing could stand in his way.

When fighting against such strongholds we need to know not only God's strength but also His strategy. Too often we become discouraged and give up because we pray and receive ministry, but because freedom and deliverance doesn't come straight away we feel even more of a failure. The Apostle Paul tells us we have the weapons, they are mighty in God; we have His power…but also need to know His plan.

We read in Psalm 103:7 that while God showed His power to the Israelites, He revealed His ways to Moses. When Joshua came up against the fortress of Jericho it must have looked impregnable but God told him how to do it and the "walls came crumbling down".

To experience God's blessing is amazing but to know how it is released and received is even better. A good friend of mine was sharing with me how as a doctor he had come to deal with the extreme stress of his work. As he sought God his prayer for immediate help was answered but God showed Him so much more. He not only gave him an answer but revealed to him a solution how to access and appropriate His peace and strength whenever he needed it. This is why a solution is even better to have than an answer. Someone can give you an answer to an equation or a sum and you can get it right, but when they show you the way to solve such problems you can get not only that one correct but all the others like it you come across. This is why prayer should never be solely going to God to get an answer or meet a problem. When we first become Christians such requests are often answered quickly, but as we grow in our faith God will sometimes delay the answers so we can develop a relationship with Him and learn His ways which are the solution to every issue of life and death.

Godly wisdom will show us the strategy, then the strategy implemented in God's power will give us the victory and the victory gives God the glory.

In one church I pastored a middle aged man who had recently come to faith in Christ asked to see me about a major problem in his life. He had experienced a very dramatic conversion and deeply loved Jesus for all He had done in his life. However, the baggage of his past sinful life was tormenting him. He had been very heavily into hard core pornography and even though he had now turned away from it the memories and images and lustful thoughts kept coming back.

I shared with him about the need to "renew his mind", which he said he had been doing by spending time in God's word and presence. There were still times, however, even during worship in church services when lustful thoughts and images would come. I suggested he start turning a negative into a positive. When the memories and lustful images came he should immediately rebuke and renounce them and pray for God's mercy and grace to deliver those he was seeing and remembering. I told him that as soon as the devil realised he was turning his attacks into opportunities to declare the power of the blood of Jesus and intercede, then he would stop using them against him.

That person is still a good friend twenty years later and serving God in his church, totally healed and free from the power of pornography and the past.

Jerusalem also became known as "The Stronghold of David", but in Psalm 27:1-3 David tells us that the real stronghold of his life and the nation is God Himself,

> *The Lord is my light and my salvation – whom shall I fear? The Lord is the **stronghold** of my life… though war break out against me, even then will I be confident.*

Psalm 27:1-3

Over the centuries, as the church grew and missionaries took the gospel to the nations, not only were people's hearts turned to God but their pagan places and temples were either demolished or their use changed. On these sites churches, cathedrals and monasteries were built. Where once there stood strongholds to spiritual darkness, now places of spiritual prayer and worship were established.

St Paul's Cathedral in London is an example of this; it sits at the top of Ludgate Hill, the highest point in the city. Long before it was built, however, there was a pagan temple dedicated on that spot to the goddess Diana which survived until King Ethelbert of Kent built the first wooden church on the site in 604AD.

The Stronghold of God's Peace

God's peace is not the absence of problems or spiritual attacks, it is His presence ruling in our hearts and minds. It is knowing that, *"In all these things we are more than conquerors,"* Romans 8:37 and *"He is able to make all things work together for good,"* Romans 8:28. This is what empowers us to rule even in the midst of our enemies. Spiritual authority is established not by trying to enforce our will but by doing God's will and knowing the peace it brings.

The devil is constantly seeking to rob us of this peace because when he does so he also steals our joy and confidence in God. In military terms we lose morale and with it our strength and ability to fight effectively. When we maintain our peace it is a crushing blow to satanic oppression and fear. Discerning where the devil is coming against us is to see where our peace and rest in God is being attacked. Where there is no peace we have strife and anxiety, but where we have victory there is peace.

When the ship Paul was sailing on to Rome was about to be destroyed by a storm he confidently reassured everyone on board to *"keep up their courage"* (Acts 27:22-23), and not lose heart because God had shown him that he would stand trial before Caesar and no one on board would die. Paul addressed the soldiers and crew on board and said that in spite of the circumstances *"I believe God, that it will happen just as He told me,"* Acts 27:25.

The more peace we have during adversity, the more we walk in Christ's victory. Such victory is not the product of our intellectual or emotional capacities, but rather trusting what God has promised will come to pass and knowing He is in total control.

Writing to the church at Philippi, the Apostle Paul said that through prayer and thanksgiving they can overcome fear and anxiety and God's peace, *"which transcends all understanding, will guard their hearts and minds in Christ Jesus"*, (Philippians 4:6-7).

According to information released by the internet company Amazon regarding searches on the Bible, this passage is the most frequently searched.

The word "guard" literally means to build a stockade and stronghold around the heart and mind.

8

Reprogramming the Brain

A Bad habit is like a comfortable bed –
Easy to get into but hard to get out of

Cricket, for many people, is already a strange sport. Part of the reason is that like many other activities or hobbies it is an acquired taste. It is for instance the only sport in which the players stop to have a cup of tea! It is built into the game and yes, it was invented in England. It is also the only sport in which one game can last for five days and you can have an exciting draw at the end of it. The longest professional game of cricket was a Test Match between South Africa and England at Durban in 1938 that lasted for ten days. It ended in an "exciting draw" as England had to leave to begin their two-day rail journey returning to their ship at Cape Town.

Here is a description of a game of cricket in which an Englishman tries to explain the sport to an American,

> You have two sides, one out in the field and one in. Each man that's in the side that's in goes out, and when he's out he comes in and the next man goes in until he's out.

When they are all out, the side that's out comes in and the side that's been in goes out and tries to get those coming in, out. Sometimes you get men still in and not out.

When a man goes out to go in, the men who are out try to get him out, and when he is out he goes in and the next man in goes out and goes in. There are two men called umpires who stay out all the time and they decide when the men who are in are out.

When both sides have been in and all the men have been out, and both sides have been out twice after all the men have been in, including those who are not out, that is the end of the game.

There are now several different formats of the game and for many the most popular is *"limited overs matches"* where each side is allotted a certain number of overs (an over is when the bowler bowls six deliveries) and the team with the highest score wins. This form of the game at international level is actually fairly recent in cricket's history. The first limited overs Cricket World Cup was in 1975 and the inaugural match was between England and India at the famous Lord's Cricket Ground. England were favourites to win, but no one could have predicted they would thrash India by 204 runs. England batted first and scored 334 for 6 wickets in their 60 overs – a respectable score. When India went in to bat they had one of the world's greatest batsmen opening their innings, Sunil Gavasker. At the time he was probably the best opening batsman in the world. Yet this was a new type of cricket for this great player and he batted throughout the innings with

"36 not out" and India scoring just 132 runs for the loss of only two wickets. The crowd (especially the Indian fans) became frustrated at the slow rate of scoring and the police had great difficulty keeping spectators off the pitch. One Indian supporter was arrested for punching a policeman and later sentenced to six months in prison.

What went wrong? Gavasker and the other Indian batsmen had difficulty changing their mind-set and the way their brains had been programmed to play cricket. In a five day test match 130 for two wickets off sixty overs was perfectly acceptable, but in this new format it was a total disaster.

Gavasker's biographer E.D.Clark writing in his book *The Record Breaking Sunil Gavasker,* says that the batsman knew he was batting badly but had a mental block and was unable to change his approach. Gavasker's cricketing brain had been programmed over many years to play in a certain way, notching up runs in the context of a five day match, but he found it impossible this day to suddenly change a lifetime's approach even when he desperately wanted to.

The expression "brain washed" is really a misnomer as the brain has not been scrubbed clean or emptied, instead it has been programmed and filled not just with new thoughts but also a new way of thinking. This, as we shall see in the next chapter, actually relates to "the mind" (how we think) rather than "the brain" (what we think). Therefore, someone who has been brain washed has had their mind radically affected.

The human brain generates more electrical impulses in a single day than all the world's telephones put together. At any one moment your brain is receiving about 100 million pieces of information which are fed into the nervous system through the ears, eyes, nose, tongue and touch receptors in the skin. However, a tiny piece of brain stem called the *reticular formation*, not much bigger than the little finger, sifts all incoming messages.

Our brains reach their full size in adolescence and begin shrinking after the age of twenty. Recent research has shown that the male brain shrinks faster than the female one, which may explain why men are more prone to problems such as memory loss.

I like the story of the man who was told by his doctor he needed a brain transplant and was offered the choice of either a male or female brain. The first cost a million pounds and the second just fifty thousand. The patient smiled and said, "I suppose the male brain is more expensive because it is superior?" "No at all," replied the surgeon, "It's because it's hardly been used."

Our brains are also able to function at a sub conscious level. Have you ever tried to think of a name or place that you are sure you know but can't remember, and then, several hours later it just pops up in your head?

Henri Fehr, the French scientist, observed that in his lifetime practically all good ideas came to him when he was not working on a problem, or even thinking about one, and that most of his contemporaries made their discoveries in the same way. When Thomas Edison was stonewalled by a problem, he would lie down, take a nap and allow his subconscious to work on it.

One night in October 1920, Frederick Grant Banting, a young Canadian surgeon with little practice who had to teach to make a living, was working on his next day's lecture. His subject was diabetes. Hour after hour he poured over the literature on this dreadful disease, his head whirling in a maze of conflicting ideas and theories, case histories and accounts of experiments with dogs. Finally, he went to bed. At two in the morning he woke up, turned on a light, and wrote down three lines in his notebook,

*   Tie off pancreatic duct of dogs

*   Wait six to eight weeks for degeneration

*   Remove residue and extract

Then he went back to bed and slept. It was those three sentences which led to the discovery of insulin. Banting's subconscious mind had come to grips with one of most baffling problems in medical science.

Habits

A researcher walked up to a little old man rocking in a chair on his porch. "I couldn't help noticing how happy you look," she said. "What's your secret for a long happy life?" "I smoke three packets of cigarettes a day," he said. "I also drink a case of whisky a week, eat fatty foods and never exercise." "That's amazing," the researcher said. "How old are you?" "Twenty-six," he replied.

For better or for worse, our habits shape us. Good habits benefit us while bad ones can destroy us. Spiritual footholds and strongholds are more than just habits, they are bondages but knowing how habits form and how they can be changed can be a practical first step in dealing with very powerful spiritual realities.

Changing Habits

There was once a man who developed the habit of checking under his bed each night to make sure no one was hiding there. After some time it became obsessive and he would wake up frequently during the night to check under his bed again and again, even though he knew no one could be there. Finally, exhausted from lack of sleep, he went to see a famous psychiatrist to see if he could break this life debilitating habit. The professor listened carefully and said he could help the man, but he would have to come twice a week for six months and it would cost £500 a session. The poor fellow said he would think about it. A week later the doctor saw the prospective patient walking down the street smiling and singing. He looked so healthy and refreshed and twenty years younger. He asked him what had happened. The man told him that after the appointment he met the janitor at his old school and told him the problem, and the old caretaker solved the problem for him immediately at no cost at all. The professor demanded to know what he said. "Oh, it was quite simple," the man replied. "The janitor said he once had the same problem and all I needed to do was go home and cut the legs off the bed!"

If only it was always that easy! It was Samuel Johnson, the famous English author and biographer who said, *"The chains of habit are too weak to be felt until they are too strong to be broken."*

It has been said that the best way to break a bad habit is to put a good habit in its place, but that habit has to be appropriate to what you are trying to replace. Experts in habit change believe it takes between twenty-one and forty days to change an unwanted habit for a desired habit.

The Power of Habit

In his book *The Power of Habit*, Charles Duhigg talks about some of the latest research by psychologists and neuroscientists on the science of habit formation. He explains how habits work in our brain. It's a bit technical but helps us to understand how habits form.

> Apparently, just beneath our grey and squiggly cerebral cortex sits a small piece of neural tissue called the *basal ganglia*. Whenever we go into "habit mode" our brain activity shifts from our higher-thinking cerebral cortex to our basal ganglia memory. It's one of the ways our brain works more efficiently.
>
> Neuroscientists have also learned that once our brain encodes a habit into our basal ganglia, that habit never really disappears. It's always there looking for that certain cue to initiate the habit sequence. That wouldn't be a problem if all our habits were good for us. Unfortunately, our brain doesn't distinguish between good habits and bad ones. It will off-load any repeated activity to the basal ganglia, even if it's to our detriment.

The Habit Loop

Duhigg calls this habit forming process "The Habit Loop" which consists of three parts,

1.   The Cue: This acts as a trigger that tells your brain to go into automatic mode and which habit to use.

2.   The Routine: This is the activity that you perform almost automatically after you encounter the cue. A routine can be physical, mental or emotional.

3.   The Reward: This is what helps our "brain figure out if (a) particular loop is worth remembering for the future." A reward can be anything from a bar of chocolate to the feeling that comes after eating a burger, smoking a cigarette or looking at pornography.

As we encounter this three-part loop over and over again, the process slowly becomes more automatic and deeply grained. What really cements the habit in our brain is when the *cue* and the *reward* work together to form powerful neurological cravings that compel us to perform the *routine*. In short, cravings are the fuel for The Habit Loop.

Here's how this happens: whenever we crave something, our brain experiences the same sort of pleasure response that we get when we actually experience a reward, whether it is eating our favourite food or some sexual gratification. But this anticipatory pleasure creates some mental discord within us because there's a conflict between what our brain feels (the pleasure of food or sex) and what we're actually experiencing (it's not actually happening right now). Our brains don't like this disconnect and will quickly close the gap by compelling us to engage in the *routine* that will give us the pleasure we're anticipating.

When something is a habit, our brain strongly associates certain *cues* with certain *rewards*. An image, a smell or even a fleeting thought trigger the desire and its fulfilment for the cravings within.

Hacking The Habit Loop to Change Bad Habits

Research has shown that by becoming aware of The Habit Loop in our lives and making simple tweaks to it we can change bad habits to good ones.

To change a habit, you must simply follow the Golden Rule of Habit Change: Keep the *cue* and *reward*; change the *routine*.

Step 1: Identify the Routine

The first step is to identify the routine you want to change in your life. Do you want to stop checking your email incessantly? Do you want to stop watching porn every night? Or maybe you want to stop your incessant worry about something bad happening?

Step 2: Experiment with the Reward

"Rewards are powerful because they satisfy cravings. But we're often not conscious of the cravings that drive our behaviours," says Duhigg. It's easy to identity our rewards – chocolate, alcohol, sexual pleasure – but what are we really craving when we go after those things? And is there a different reward that will satisfy the true craving but in a more positive way?

Step 3: Identify the Cue

Once you identify the reward, it's time to identify the cue: the thing that triggers the craving. What causes the desire and drives you to fulfil it?

Step 4: Create a Plan

After you identify the cue and reward you can start making plans to change your routine. According to researchers, the best way to plan your habit change is through implementation intentions.

This is how the above steps work out in practice. If for instance you constantly worry about your health the routine would be to keep checking endlessly to make sure there is nothing wrong with you. The reward from doing this would be to have peace of mind that you are well and nothing bad is going to happen. The cue that triggers the craving could be a traumatic illness you have had in the past. It could be a history of sickness in your family. It might be the fear of what would happen to those you love if you were ill and so forth. You cannot change what has happened to you in the past or your family's history so the cue will always be there and so will the need to have peace of mind and reassurance. The key to break this fear filled habit is to change the routine. So instead of constant checking and searching the internet about physical symptoms you find your peace in God and not in Google, (internet search engine). Thank God that He is sovereign and in control of everything that has happened to you or will happen. Rest in His grace and love knowing that, *"In all things God works for the good of those who love Him, who have been called according to His purpose,"* Romans 8:28.

Or maybe the habit is pornography. One statistic I read stated that this is the second most common use of the internet after researching for medical symptoms. The reward can be pleasure, power and so forth. The cue (what triggers the craving) may be the need for fantasy and escapism, loneliness, medicating your pain, gratifying your physical needs and cravings etc. Breaking the habit and bondage begins by recognising its evil and destructiveness and determining to find joy and well-being in God. Therefore to change the routine instead of turning to porn when lonely and hurting we stop and seek God's presence, where there is both healing and fullness of joy. Let the image of the cross fill our thoughts and thank Him for such amazing love. And come before God's throne of grace to receive mercy and find grace to help in our time of need, Hebrews 4:16.

The battle will be over what maximises your pleasure and medicates your pain.

Step 5: Believe You Can Change

A final ingredient necessary for lasting habit change is to believe that change is possible. Researchers have found that the best way to foster that belief in yourself is to surround yourself with a supportive group of people.

The ability of groups to encourage belief that change is possible is one of the reasons researchers believe organisations such as *Alcoholics Anonymous* (AA) has been so successful with helping people beat their alcohol habit.

Your group doesn't have to be large. In fact, just having one other person to turn to as you change your habit can foster the belief that you can change your bad habit. Find an accountability partner that you can meet with on a regular basis to report on your progress and get encouragement from.

Two thousand years ago the Apostle Paul understood that real life transforming change takes place when we replace what brings death with that which brings life.

> *You were taught, with regard to your former way of life, to put off your old self, which is being corrupted by its deceitful desires; to be made new in the attitude of your minds; and to put on the new self, created to be like God in true righteousness and holiness.*

> *Therefore each of you must put off falsehood and speak truthfully to his neighbour.*

> *In your anger do not sin, Do not let the sun go down while you are still angry, and do not give the devil a foothold.*

> *He who has been stealing must steal no longer, but must work, doing something useful with his own hands, that he may have something to share with those in need.*

> *Do not let any unwholesome talk come out of your mouths, but only what is helpful for building others up according to their needs, that it may benefit those who listen.*

> Ephesians 4:22-29

9

Renewing the Mind

Do not conform to the pattern of this world,
but be transformed by the renewing of your mind.
Romans 12:2

Both caterpillars and chameleons are fascinating in their different ways. The first because from a struggling shrivelled cocoon a beautiful butterfly is able to emerge and soar into the sky. The other because of their ability to blend into the background and be absorbed by their environment. When the Apostle Paul tells us not to be conformed to this world but to be transformed by the *"renewing of our mind",* he is warning us not to become a spiritual and a social chameleon, indistinguishable from the world and controlled by it, rather, we are to be like the butterfly that emerges out of the cocoon changed and transformed.

We are saved to affect the world, not to reflect it. This is what the word Holy means; to be set apart from something and for something, to be different. The church of Jesus is called to be a counter culture not a sub culture of this world. A chameleon keeps changing to fit into the environment but a caterpillar changes to be transformed from it.

113

While our brain is an amazing creation, the mind is even more incredible. The mind is spiritual, the brain, however, is just physical. While the brain can be reprogrammed to help form new habits and patterns, true freedom only comes with the mind being renewed. This is because the brain is about what we think, but the mind is about the way we think, how we process information, formulate our understanding and interpret the data. This is why the devil doesn't attack our brain he attacks our minds, *"The god of this age has blinded the minds of unbelievers,"* 2 Corinthians 4:4. It's also the reason why knowing Jesus as saviour and Lord is never simply by academic ability or intellectual learning, God says, *"I will put my laws in their minds and write them on their hearts,"* Jeremiah 31:33. We do not have the brain of Jesus, what we have is the mind of Christ; we do not have all His knowledge but we can think the way He thinks through His Spirit at work within us.

The mind is one of God's greatest gifts to man and by this we are able to rule over our natural world. We are not the biggest, strongest or fastest, but we can be the wisest, the cleverest and the smartest.

The mind is also closely connected to our spirit, because of this, only humans can worship God. Animals have a brain and you can teach a monkey to lift its hands or a horse to dance and a gorilla to bow down, but these will never be acts of worship.

Our next door neighbour sometimes keeps his parrot in a cage in his porch opposite our front door. It is excellent at mimicking the sound of our telephone ringing and also my wife's voice and Welsh accent by saying "I'm home!" Many a time I have answered back only to find I was having a conversation with the bird.

I heard of a lady who taught her parrot hymns and choruses, often people would come and listen to the bird perform and the owner would pass around a mission box for offerings. The bird could sing but it was never worship, because worship involves our spirit, John 4:24. It did however help to support several missionaries and raise more money for Christian work than many Christians.

In Ephesians 4:23 we are told to be *"Renewed in the spirit of your mind."* The Greek is in the present continuous tense, meaning a process that needs to keep on happening as we submit our lives to God. It also reveals that the mind has a spiritual element to it.

Commenting on this, Dr Martyn Lloyd Jones says,

> The spirit of our mind refers to an interior principle, a guiding, driving, directing power that governs and operates the mind itself. It is apart from and in addition to our mental and intellectual faculties. Paul is referring not simply to the abilities of the human brain but rather to that power that directs and controls those abilities.

The very fact the mind needs to be "renewed" implies something has gone wrong and we need to be brought back to how God originally intended it to be. Paul is saying that one of the most devastating effects of sin is that the spirit of our minds went wrong. When man listened to the devil he put himself under his dominion and the result is that his mind has come under alien domination.

The god of this age has blinded the minds of unbelievers, so that they cannot see the light of the gospel of the glory of Christ, who is the image of God.

2 Corinthians 4:4

Note, it is the spirit of the mind that is gone wrong, not the brain as an instrument of learning, but rather our fundamental way of thinking and reasoning has become twisted and perverted.

Woe to those who call evil good and good evil, who put darkness for light and light for darkness, who put bitter for sweet and sweet for bitter.

Isaiah 5:20

This kind of thinking was evident at the trial of a well-known celebrity in the UK recently when one of his ex-mistresses told the court that the defendant was honest and upright because he had told her from the beginning of their affair he would not leave his wife.

Here is another quote that illustrates how abnormal some thinking can become,

I haven't committed a crime. What I did was fail to comply with the law.

David Dinkins, New York City Mayor, answering accusations that he failed to pay his taxes.

The Scriptures do not deny man's ability to think, but rather the manner of thinking has become affected by sin. A person may have a brilliant intellect but reach the wrong conclusions because of erroneous presuppositions and fallacious reasoning. This is known by theologians as the *noetic* effects of sin.

The word the Bible often uses to describe a person who refuses to believe in God is *fool,* Psalm 14:1. The meaning of this word is primarily a moral not mental problem. It describes a person whose reasoning and "how" to think has become distorted.

When we grasp this, we will never be surprised why intellectuals, scientists and scholars are not Christians and deny the God who made them.

The best that scientist Albert Einstein could conclude was that there must be something, some power, behind the universe. He did not believe in a personal God but he was quick to point out that he was no atheist, he wrote,

> In view of such harmony in the cosmos which I, with my limited human mind, am able to recognize, there are yet people who say there is no God. But what really makes me angry is that they quote me for the support of such views. 1

> I'm not an atheist and I don't think I can call myself a pantheist. We are in the position of a little child entering a huge library filled with books in many languages. The child knows someone must have written those books. It does not know how. It does not understand the languages in which they are written. The child dimly suspects a mysterious order in the arrangements of the books, but doesn't know what it is. That, it seems to me, is the attitude of even the most intelligent human being toward God. 2

In my previous books, *The Captured Heart* and *Issues of the Heart,* I have pointed out that what someone thinks is not only determined by the information they receive but also by how they interpret it.

Most people like to believe that they make intelligent and rational decisions, but what we don't always realise is the extent to which our nature and disposition influences what we think because it affects how we think. You cannot separate the thinking processes from the content and character of the heart. This is why the terms for the heart and the mind are often used interchangeably in Scripture (see appendix A). What we think is in our heads but the way we think is in our hearts. This is why God writes His laws on our mind and hearts, Hebrews 8:10. It's also the reason we are told,

*For from within, out of men's **hearts**, come evil thoughts.*

Mark 7:21

*As a man thinks in his **heart** so is he.*

Proverbs 23:7

*The fool says in his **heart,** there is no God.*

Psalm 14:1

How we think is influenced by a combination of our convictions, experiences, upbringing, environment, education, nature and culture. These form the passions and priorities, pride and prejudices, values and virtues, we carry in our hearts, and become the filters through which we process information and they control the way we think. Many people believe they are logically thinking through issues when in reality all they are doing is rearranging their preferences and prejudices.

This is why two equally gifted and intelligent politicians will look at the same data, analyse the same issues and come to completely opposite opinions. It's why two sports fans supporting opposing teams will see the same incident and one will cry foul while the other says the person dived or just fell over.

It's also the reason why two brilliant scientists will look at creation and one will say it is all the product of chance while the other insists there must be a creator. Atheists come to their conclusions because they filter what they think through the prism of how they think in their heart.

A good example of this is the following statement made by Dr Paul Davies, a physicist and atheist who argues for a creation without God,

> The origin of life is a stubbornly enduring mystery. How can a collection of chemicals form themselves into a living thing without any interference from outside? On the face of it life is an exceedingly unlikely event and there is no known principle that matter says it has to organise itself into life. I'm very happy to believe in my head that we live in a bio friendly universe, because in my heart I find that very congenial. But we have not discovered the life principle. 3

He says, "I can live with something there is no evidence for in my head because in my heart I find it suits me." Dr Duane Gish, a leading creation scientist, was right when he pointed out, "It's incredible what an unbeliever must believe to be an unbeliever."

The atheist Richard Dawkins in his book *The God Delusion* reveals the same flaws in his reasoning because in his heart he desperately wants there to be no God. He admits that "Jesus was a great ethical motivator" but does not believe He redeemed mankind. However, Jesus claimed to have come to forgive sin and redeem us, so you can see the contradiction Dawkins has when he says that Jesus was a man of great ethical integrity and at the same time He deceived those who followed Him?

A few years ago Dawkins was debating the Rev Giles Fraser, former Canon Chancellor of St Paul's Cathedral, on BBC Radio 4. Dawkins' *Foundation for Reason and Science* had claimed that Christians in Britain tend to be more secular then the "Christian lobbyists" who speak on their behalf. He claimed evidence for this in a poll that showed many who identified themselves as Christian could not name basic aspects of Christianity and were therefore not Christian.

Canon Fraser countered by asking Dawkins to state the full title of Charles Darwin's book *Origin of Species*, otherwise, Fraser argued using Dawkins' reasoning, Dawkins was not truly an evolutionist-believing atheist.

The next few minutes were quite hilarious and very revealing as Dawkins had several attempts to name the full title. In his desperation not to look foolish and give the complete title he even had an "Oh God" moment when he said, "Uh…With, oh, God, Um..."

It was an astonishing, highly significant moment when a militant atheist who has been called the "High Pope of Darwinism", inadvertently called upon the God he vehemently denies to help him name the book he has built much of his life and belief upon. The full title that Dawkins never managed to name is *On the Origin of Species by Means of Natural Selection, or the Preservation of Favoured Races in the Struggle for Life.*

Francis S. Collins is one of the world's leading scientists. He is noted for his landmark discoveries of diseased genes and his leadership of the Human Genome Project. He is also the director of the National Human Genome Research Institute. In his book *The Language of God: A Scientist Presents Evidence for Belief* (2006), he tells of his intellectual and moral journey from atheism to faith in Christ. He states that all his scientific discoveries are now an "opportunity to worship".

We do not need a new brain to become a Christian, the one we have will do fine, but we do need a new heart and a new spirit, which enables us to be *"renewed in the spirit of our mind."*

> *"This is the covenant I will make with the house of Israel after that time," declares the Lord. "I will put my law in their minds and write it on their hearts. I will be their God, and they will be my people."*

Jeremiah 31:33

The famous former slave trader John Newton once saw the slaves of Africa and the West Indies as sub human commodities for pleasure and profit. Then he had a life changing encounter with God who wrote His laws on Newton's heart and mind. After that he saw those same men and women completely differently. He did all he could to support William Wilberforce to abolish the evil slave trade. His change of mind was because of his change of heart.

Three Forms of Knowing

There are basically three forms of knowledge;

* Mathematical understanding which is typified by logic. Two plus two will always equal four, unless you cannot add up!

* Scientific or experimental knowledge which is expressed by laws through repeatable observable experiment.

* Personal or experiential knowledge which finds its highest expression in what we call "love". This is quite different from the other two and is the deepest and most meaningful knowing of all.

When we try to express something personal in scientific or mathematical terms it can become a very poor representation of the real thing, as is seen in a scientific textbook that described a kiss as "the approach of two pairs of lips with reciprocal transmission of microbes and carbon dioxide." Mathematically and scientifically correct, but try telling that to two people in love.

When it comes to knowing God, scientific and mathematical knowledge is not enough. They can help us to know about Him but God is not a principle, a power or a philosophy, He is a person and to know Him involves personal and experiential knowledge. This is why we are told to love God with all our heart, mind and strength. It is also why in the Bible *"to know"* is never simply understanding facts or memorizing texts. It means to have a personal understanding and relationship.

When Jesus says, *"You shall know the truth and the truth shall set you free,"* He is not saying all you have to do is memorise texts or believe facts, but rather to enter into a relationship with Himself who is the truth.

I have been married to my wife, Jan, for more than thirty years, but I have known her and about her for more than 40 years. We went to the same junior and senior schools and were in the same class. I tell people that for the first ten years we never had a single argument because we never spoke to each other. We never fell out because we never fell in. In fact, I cannot remember speaking to her all the time we were in school.

A few years after we left school we ended up in the same church and that was when I got to know her. Before that I could tell you mathematically and scientifically about her. I knew how tall she was, what colour hair she had, she was very intelligent and slim. I didn't know her, however, until we spent time together and I began to open my heart to her and she opened her heart to me.

The reason why many atheists have such a problem with believing in God is that while they have understanding of the first two forms of knowledge they are in ignorance concerning this personal knowing.

Renewing the Mind

We renew the mind with *truth*. But what is *the truth*? Pilate asked Jesus this question and couldn't see that "the truth" was standing in front of him. God's word is truth, God's Spirit is the Spirit of Truth, Jesus is "the Truth" and the Father's Kingdom is a kingdom of "Truth".

We will never know victory in our life until we walk in victory in our minds. I am so grateful to the late Tom Marshall for much of the following which he teaches in his excellent book *Free Indeed*. He says,

> The mind of man remains the strategic battleground in the universe. The struggle to dominate the mind is the struggle to dominate man himself. Christians today must understand clearly the function of the human mind, the problem it faces and – most important of all – the provision God has made for its redemption.

Marshall goes on to show that the sources of our thought life come from three distinct arenas.

The World

A lot of our natural world is morally neutral, such as the weather or colour clothes we wear. But the world also has another connotation and is spoken of in Scripture as a system of living and believing that is alienated and hostile to God. It includes the media, politics, films, the economic system and daily we are exposed to its outlooks, opinions and propaganda. Satan is described as *"the god of this world"*, (2 Corinthians 4:4).

The Flesh

When used in its moral or spiritual sense "the flesh" does not mean the human body. It is the world within, rather than the world without, the internal rather than the external environment. In the New Testament the flesh is the sum of all the desires, appetites, needs and drives that make for self-gratification. Through The Fall it has become the principle of sin in man, Romans 7:2-23, James 1:14,15, Romans 8:7,8.

For the flesh to be gratified it has to capture the mind. Every sin, as Jesus pointed out in the Sermon on the Mount, is first a sin of the mind (and heart).

The Devil

Satan has access to the mind of man through the world and the flesh. Whether we like it or not, it is part of the situation into which we have been born. He uses this access to plant temptations in our minds (Matthew 4 and Luke 4.) We are not responsible for them because they did not originate within us, but we are responsible if we harbour and fulfil them.

Even after conversion there can still be many bondages in the mind. In this condition, although the mind is open to revelation of divine truth and the promptings of the Holy Spirit, it is also open to other things as well. Old thought patterns and temptations surprise us by their persistence and wear us down into a state of defeat and despair.

Marshall says,

> God's provision to meet every need of the human race is always found in two divine works or actions, the cross and the work of the Holy Spirit, both are essential and go together...On the cross Jesus yielded Himself to the power of darkness (Luke 22:53), but by His death and resurrection He shattered that power forever over all the lives identified with Him. The cross operates to render ineffective all the enslaving authorities that have taken charge of our minds. For the work Jesus did on the cross to become effective in our life it has to be personally appropriated.

The cross of Jesus deals not only with forgiveness but also with deliverance. This must also be personally appropriated and it is the only way we can be set free from the domination of the authorities that rule in our minds.

To do this we need to:

1. Confess the sins of our mind and receive God's forgiveness.

2. Renounce and reject the authority that, in our mind, we have given to the world, the flesh, the past and the devil. Make the act of renunciation very specific and definite – confess it aloud until you really know in your heart it has been done.

Satan, I renounce you and all your works. In the name of Jesus I reject the hold of fear and the ungodly thoughts and control you have on my mind, because your authority was rendered powerless at Calvary. I take back right now every inch of ground I have yielded in my mind to fear and I bring all my thoughts under the Lordship of Jesus Christ.

Receiving a Renewed Mind

In the renewal of the mind it is the cross and the power of the resurrection that breaks the power of the authorities that once ruled there and it is the Holy Spirit who renews our liberated mind. As we yield our minds to the Holy Spirit He will wash out the old habitual thought patterns, compulsive thoughts and the weary treadmill of negativity. The bondage is broken, the curse is lifted and the mind is free. It is a mind in which there is only now one authority because *thoughts have been brought back captive to Jesus.* Paul calls this in Romans 8:6 *"a mind set on the spirit".* Because the internal problem of authority has been resolved the result is life and peace.

Those who live according to the sinful nature have their minds set on what that nature desires; but those who live in accordance with the Spirit have their minds set on what the Spirit desires. The mind of sinful man is death, but the mind controlled by the Spirit is life and peace.

Romans 8:5,6

When an alien thought intrudes its true source is readily manifested, no matter how plausible it seems, because peace is disturbed. Deal with the intruder and peace reigns again.

Retaining a Renewed Mind

The renewing of the mind is not only a crisis but a process, Romans 12:2. A necessity of our human nature is that we need not only to be made free but to learn how to use freedom to remain free, (Galatians 5:13).

When your mind is renewed, from then on you decide what is going to occupy it. Some people have become so accustomed to a mind which claims autonomy that it comes as something of a surprise to find that we (and not our minds) are to determine what our minds think about (Philippians 4:8). The renewal of the mind does not exempt us from temptation. Jesus' victory on the cross does not prevent the devil's attacks against us but it does destroy his power over us.

Therefore, the temptation of itself is not the real problem. The real problem is the place of authority that the temptation has in our minds. This is what makes the task of ejecting unwanted thoughts so difficult. Once we settle the question of authority victory becomes an exciting reality.

Once we have said the irrevocable "yes" to the Lordship of Christ in our minds, the renewing work of the Holy Spirit becomes a continuous experience. A mirror can reflect only what it beholds – even so we can only reflect in our lives as much of Christ as we can see – what we behold of Christ is determined by what we receive through the revelation of the Holy Spirit.

There are many things we can do to relax and refresh our mind which can be beneficial, but only God's Spirit and truth are able to renew our minds.

> *The mind governed by the flesh is death, but the mind governed by the Spirit is life and peace.*

Romans 8:6

Francis Frangipane writes in his book *The Three Battle Grounds,*

> The place Jesus was crucified was called Golgotha, the place of the skull. To be effective in spiritual warfare we must learn warfare in the battle ground of the mind – the place of the skull. The territory of the uncrucified thought life is the beach head of satanic assault in our lives. To defeat the devil we must be crucified in the place of the skull. We must be renewed in the spirit of our minds.

1 Prinz Hubertus zu Lowenstein, Towards the Further Shore; An autobiography, Victor Gollancz, London, 1968, p. 156.

2 G. S. Viereck, Glimpses of the Great (Macauley, New York, 1930), quoted by D. Brian, Einstein: A Life , p. 186.

3 Joel Achenbach, *Life Beyond Earth, National Geographic*, January 2000,

10

Resetting The Heart

Since, then, you have been raised with Christ,
set your hearts on things above, where Christ
is seated at the right hand of God.

Colossians 3:1

In a lecture on the importance of "guarding your heart" Professor Wayne Grudem, who is one of the world's foremost Biblical scholars today, tells a story about the famous theologian, Professor Charles Hodge. Hodge sought to understand why a nation like Germany which gave us Martin Luther and the Reformation, also gave the world "higher criticism and theological liberalism" which deny the truthfulness of the Bible and many Christian doctrines.

As Professor of Oriental and Biblical Literature (and later of Systematic Theology) at Princeton Seminary from 1820 –1878, Hodge decided to go and study in Germany for two years and returned to Princeton in 1828. On his return he gave a lecture to the seminary asking how it was that in the former great centres of Protestantism, especially Germany, Christianity had ceased to be even the nominal religion.

Hodge, one of the foremost theologians of the nineteenth century, said that the cause was the decline of what he referred to as "vital religion". He told the students and the faculty,

> Holiness is essential to the correct knowledge of divine things and the great security from error. Wherever you find vital piety, there you find the doctrines of the fall, of depravity, of regeneration, of atonement, and of the deity of Jesus Christ. 1

Hodge then exhorted the seminary students, *"keep your hearts with all diligence, for out of them are the issues of life"* (Proverbs 4:23). He told them, "Holiness is essential to correct knowledge of divine things, and the great security from error. When men lose the life of religion, they can believe the most monstrous doctrines, and glory in them." When the heart is captured by evil and error the mind can come to most erroneous and demonic conclusions.

During an average lifetime the human heart will beat more than two billion times – each beat pushing blood around the body 1,440 times a day. In one hour, the heart works hard enough to produce the equivalent energy needed to raise almost one ton in weight three feet off the ground.

But while the heart is incredibly strong it can also be very fragile. This is true spiritually as well as physically and emotionally. The heart can be courageous and crushed, brave and broken, pure and polluted, a treasure or a traitor. This is why we are warned to *"...above all else guard our hearts for from it flows the issues of life,"* Proverbs 4:23.

What the devil seeks most is our heart, and what God desires above all else is for us to love Him with all our heart.

Therefore, the heart (and mind) is the great battleground for the souls of men and women. You will often hear it said in a social-political context that the real battle is for the "hearts and minds" of the people.

In his book *Walking with God,* John Eldredge describes some of the battles he has had in fighting for his own heart in dealing with lingering and long standing disappointments in his life.

> As I was praying about my disappointments the other day, I noticed something lingering beneath the surface. I realized somewhere along the way, I'd come to an agreement of sorts – *I need this*. Not just that I want it, and very much, but that *I need it*. It's a very subtle and deadly shift. One that opens the door to despair and a host of other enemies. I was coming to believe that God's love and God's life are not enough.
>
> We start out longing for something, and the more we come to believe this is what we have to have to be happy, the more we obsess about it. The prize just out of reach swells far beyond its actual meaning. It begins to take on mythic proportions. We are certain life will come together once we achieve this. We think if only I was married, or if only I had children, if only I was rich, if only I was thinner or stronger or fitter or healthier etc and everything else in our lives pales into comparison. Even God. We are falling to believe we *need* whatever is just beyond our reach and when we fall to this we are miserable.
>
> I am not minimizing the disappointment. The ache is real. What I am saying is the

disappointment and ache swells beyond its nature, dominates the landscape of our psyche when we shift from *'how I long for this'* to *'I need this.'*

The only thing we truly need in life is God and the life He gives us. There is a satisfaction we don't want to come to until we come to it in God.

This shift I've been describing, this coming to believe that what I don't have and have been longing for I actually *need* is the opening stages of the disaster. For whatever reason we have come to believe at God is not enough.

And so whatever else might be the reasons for our disappointments, there is no question that God uses them to draw us to Himself. To wean our hearts from every other perceived source of life, so that we might come to find our life in Him.

I know that I face a choice. I can feel down inside and I watch it take place in my heart. I can let my disappointments define my life. Or I can let them take me back to God, to find my life in Him in ways I have not yet learned. The rest remains a mystery. But this is enough to know.

And so I break the agreement that I've made that I 'need' this. I give this place in my heart back to you, God, fill me with your love and your life, in this very place, Amen.

One of my favourite films is *Cool Runnings.* It is loosely-based on the real-life story of the first Jamaican bobsled team to enter the Olympics. It's a fun movie of four Jamaicans who've never even seen snow before travelling to Canada for the 1988 Winter Games in Calgary.

Amazingly, in the film they qualify for the final and are in with a good chance of a medal. Derice, the captain of the team, had dreamed of winning an Olympic medal. In his mind, he believed that if he could do that one thing, his whole life would be deemed successful. When he didn't qualify in the 100-metre sprint to compete with the Jamaican team in the Summer Olympics, he turned his attention to bobsledding. He was so singularly focused on what he thought was important that he began to forget who he was. He began to alienate his team mates and tried to be something he wasn't.

The night before the final the film shows him sitting in his room going over the course layout. Irv, the team coach who had been a great bobsled champion but was disgraced because he cheated to win an Olympic gold, comes into the room and asks Derice if he needs anything, he answers, yes, there is one thing: he needs to know why Irv cheated. Irv doesn't hold back.

"It's a fair question; it's quite simple, really – I had to win. You see, Derice, I had made winning my whole life, and when you make winning your whole life, you have to keep on winning, no matter what. Understand?"

Derice responds, "No, I don't understand. You won two gold medals. You had it all."

Irv replies, "Derice, a gold medal is a wonderful thing; but if you're not enough without it, you'll never be enough with it."

Derice asks, "Hey coach, how will I know if I'm enough?"

Irv answers, "When you cross that finish line, you'll know."

The next day in the race the sled's steering broke and the team crashed resulting in them coming last. But that didn't matter, they were unhurt and so they picked up the bobsled and carried it to the finishing line with the crowds applauding and cheering.

The person who says they will never be happy and at peace until they have the perfect job, or pastor a large church, or have a certain amount of money in the bank, is establishing a power in their heart that says "I need this". Maybe you have said "when my spouse changes" or "when I reach a certain weight" or "when I am properly recognised and appreciated for all my abilities," that's when you will be fulfilled and secure. What you are saying is, "I need this", and in doing so you are giving that desire great power over you.

I am not saying it is wrong to have dreams and desires, however, we have to be careful about what we set our heart and mind on and make sure that they are subject to what should be the greatest passion in our lives – loving God with all our heart, soul, strength and mind.

The only way to be truly free is to give everything to Jesus and make Him Lord of our lives. Everything we hold onto for ourselves has the potential to capture us and be used against us. When we put it all in His hands that's when we find life and peace. Take for example our loved ones, even they can be the cause of fear and pain. We can fret about something bad happening to them or "what are they up to now?" and that becomes an entry point of anxiety and even torment that the devil uses. Or take the issues of our money and possessions.

When we think we are in control of them they are often controlling us. We can become dominated in the pursuit for more or terrified of losing what we have.

It's when we put everything in God's hands that life and peace begin to flow.

A good friend of mine, a former CEO of a major Christian book company, told me of a meeting he was invited to in London of Christian business people. Some of those present were very wealthy and heads of well-known family food dynasties. One lady shared very openly about the stresses and pressures of heading up such a large corporation. After she finished speaking another gentlemen stood up who was the owner of another major food empire and told everyone how he had found the answer to being responsible for so much money and his corporation. He said, "I gave it all away." Some of those present looked shocked, and he then explained what he meant. He told them, "I gave it all to Jesus. I put all the wealth, the company, the future in His hands. And now He helps me run His business and it's wonderful."

How Are You Medicating Your Pain?

When Nelson Mandela was released from his tiny cell on the notorious Robben Island in South Africa on February 11, 1990, he had spent 27 years in prison; many people had campaigned for his freedom. What most of the watching world didn't know, however, was the fight Mandela had won in his own heart to be free not just on the outside but even more importantly within himself. It was winning this battle that made him into the great leader and statesman he became and helped to prevent a nation from destroying itself. He says of that momentous day,

> As I walked out the door toward my freedom I
> knew that if I did not leave all the anger,
> hatred and bitterness behind I would still be
> in prison.

American psychiatrist and author, Scott Peck, begins his bestselling book *The Road Less Travelled* with a sentence just three words long, "Life is difficult". He says that from the moment we are born we leave behind the warm and safe environment that has nourished us for nine months and out into the cold we are thrust – into the glaring lights, turned upside down and smacked…welcome to the world.

> For many life ends difficult; old age, poverty,
> sickness and disease and every day in between
> can have some degree of difficulty. So, very early
> on, we learn to soothe and medicate our pain.
> We cry till our mother comes and feeds and
> holds us. We suck our thumbs, hide under our
> blankets and as we grow we find more socially
> advanced ways of dealing with pain – becoming
> the extrovert that everyone likes or maybe an
> introvert to prevent anyone getting too close. It
> may be achieving good grades, making people
> laugh, pumping iron in the gym or dressing
> smart to get compliments. Or perhaps, Peck
> says, it is like people he has counselled and wept
> with, who cut themselves and mutilate their
> bodies because the physical pain is easier to
> cope with than the emotional anguish that
> overwhelms them.

It doesn't end there though because this world offers us a myriad other ways of dealing with pain; the chemical solution of nicotine or heroin, or maybe downing a bottle of wine or several beers, perhaps popping a box of chocolates. For some it's sex and looking at porn and maybe indulging in it. Others drive fast, pump adrenalin and fill their life with activity.

But when all is said and done the pain is merely numbed for a while and always returns. It is here we have to be honest and admit we don't only need natural help but supernatural intervention. It's the "God moment" when spirituality enters in. Richard Rohr, an international author and retreat leader, says, "Spirituality is all about what you do with your pain." You can choose to medicate it, or you can face it in God's presence and know His healing and wholeness.

Henri Nouwen once said,

> I cannot continuously say 'No' to this or 'No' to that, unless there is something ten times more attractive to choose. Saying 'No' to my lust, my greed, my needs, and the world's powers takes an enormous amount of energy. The only hope is to find something so obviously real and attractive that I can devote all my energies to saying 'Yes'...One such thing I can say 'Yes' to is when I come in touch with the fact that I am loved. Once I have found that in my total brokenness I am still loved, I become free from the compulsion of doing successful things.

Something miraculous happens when people connect with God's love, we discover that He is the lover and the healer of our souls. It doesn't matter how much brokenness and how many pieces there are, He can make us whole when we give them, and most of all ourselves, to Him. This is where healing and freedom begins, it is not only the giving of our pain and bondage but the surrender of our lives to Him who is the source of all life. For while our minds are renewed by God's

Word and truth, our hearts are reset through our worship and surrender.

1 David B. Calhoun, *Princeton Seminary: Vol.1: Faith and Learning, 1812 - 1868* (Edinburgh and Carlisle, Pennsylvania: Banner of Truth, 1994, p. 123)

11

Reviving the Spirit

Those who hope in the Lord, will renew their strength. They will soar on wings like eagles, they will run and not grow weary, they will walk and not faint.

Isaiah 40:31

Some years ago a Christian magazine carried the fascinating account of a Church of Christ minister who had been presumed dead and was then reunited with his family after sixteen years.

The reunion came after James Simmons, preaching in a Baptist church in Texas, was recognized by a former parishioner as Wesley Barret "Barre" Cox, who had mysteriously disappeared in 1984. Simmons was reunited with his mother and brother on New Year's Day, his sister-in-law Mary Cox told the Associated Press. He did not recognize his relatives, but she immediately knew him from his looks, his voice and his demeanour, she said, "It was just a blessing to see him and to hug him, it was just the answer to our prayers. We're happy for (his mother) because she never did give up on the fact that he was alive."

Simmons was 33 and married with a six-month-old daughter when he disappeared while a minister at MacArthur Park

Church of Christ in San Antonio. His vandalized car was found abandoned near Abilene, Texas. When an extensive search provided no clues to where he was, his wife, Beth Cox, eventually presumed him dead. She moved to California and then Franklin, Tennessee.

Wesley Cox (James Simmons), had however, been brutally beaten, then left for dead in the boot of a car and as a result totally lost his memory. After he recovered physically, he returned to his ministry roots, turning up at the Golden Gate Baptist Theological Seminary in Mill Valley, California. He told the seminary he had created a new identity and life since his attack and had no memory of anything that went before. He earned a master of divinity degree in 1994 and a master of theology degree in 1999 and earned several student recognition awards.

What is so amazing about this story is not only his reuniting with his family and the answers to their prayers, but also with no memory of his past life he once again chose to become a minister of the gospel. Even though his brain had been damaged by the assault and memory of all his past life was destroyed he still loved the Lord Jesus and in his spirit sought to serve and follow Him.

We are far more than the sum of our brains' intellectual attainments and memories or of our hearts' emotional responses and capacities. While we live in a body and have a soul (mind, will and emotions) we are primarily a spirit, and it is our human spirit that ultimately defines who we are and what we become.

In Romans 12:1,2, Paul tells us to present to God our bodies as living sacrifices and to renew our minds. Jesus says the greatest commandment is to love God with all our heart, mind, soul and strength. We must be spiritual beings to be able to do this and for this. It is from our spirit that we determine to present our body and desire to love God and renew our mind. For we are not primarily physical beings on a spiritual journey but spiritual beings on a physical journey.

This is also why we are never defeated by what happens to us physically, emotionally or mentally but it is when our spirit becomes overpowered and crushed.

You may have heard the proverb that says *"a cheerful heart is like good medicine"* but it goes on to say *"a crushed spirit dries up the bones"*, Proverbs 17:22. There is another Proverb that tells us, *"A man's spirit sustains him in sickness but a crushed spirit who can bear?"* Proverbs 18:14. We can endure all kinds of physical and emotional affliction but when our spirit is bruised and damaged we lose the strength to fight and carry on.

There are so many ways our spirit can become damaged and wounded; usually it is either by something sinful done by us or to us. Sin is whatever comes between us and God and is the curse of humanity. When King David committed adultery with Bathsheba his momentary pleasure caused him to lose his joy and strongholds of deception and death became a part of his life. He cried out to God in brokenness and repentance,

> *Create in me a pure heart, O God, and renew a steadfast spirit within me. Do not cast me from your presence or take your Holy Spirit from me.*

Restore to me the joy of your salvation and grant me a willing spirit, to sustain me.

Psalm 51:10-12

Four times in his letters Paul prays for the churches that, *"The grace of the Lord Jesus Christ be with your spirit."* And he tells Timothy,

For God did not give us a spirit of timidity, but a spirit of power, of love and of self-discipline.

2 Timothy 1:7

Paul writes to the church at Ephesus,

I pray that out of his glorious riches he may strengthen you with power through his Spirit in your inner being,

Ephesians 3:16

A Prayer for healing

The Lord is close to the broken hearted and saves those who are crushed in spirit.

Psalm 34:18

Heavenly Father, I come to you in the Name of the Lord Jesus Christ. You know everything that I have done and all that has ever happened to me. I choose to forgive all those who have spoken negatively to me and about me. I forgive those who have hurt me and I surrender and submit all my hurts and wounding to you. I now consciously forgive all those who have spoken negatively and done hurtful things to me and to those whom I love.

I release my wounded spirit to you to be healed in the mighty name of Jesus. I receive your mercy and grace, your forgiveness and your joy, your peace and your blessing, your health and your strength, and your wholeness and your presence into my spirit right now.

Thank you for healing and restoring me and I command all footholds and strongholds of pain and defeat to be demolished and destroyed and for your strongholds of love and life to be established in their place. Amen.

STRONGHOLD BUSTERS

Footholds and Strongholds

Stronghold Busters

I mentioned earlier in the book that it is reckoned to take up to forty days to break an old habit and replace it with a new one. This number forty also has significant Biblical meaning and associations.

- When God wanted to cleanse the world it rained for forty days and forty nights, Genesis 7:12.

- Moses spent forty days and nights on the mountain with God when he was being given the commands for the nation to live by, Exodus 24:18, 28-29.

- The twelve spies took forty days to search out the Promised Land (one day for each of the forty years they were in the wilderness) Numbers 13:25.

- Goliath taunted and tormented the Israelite army for forty days before being killed by David, 1 Samuel 17:16.

- Elijah was strengthened by an angelic meal after he was threatened by Jezebel, and travelled for forty days to Mount Horeb where he met with God, 1 Kings 19:8.

- Jonah warned the city of Nineveh that the people had forty days until God would judge them. They repented in those forty days and God spared the city, Jonah 3:4 and 10.

- Jesus fasted for forty days in the wilderness and overcame Satan's temptations, Matthew 4:1-12.

- Jesus was seen in the earth forty days after His crucifixion, Acts 1:3.

One of the titles used for Satan in the Bible is Beelzebub, it means *"lord of the flies"*, Matthew 12:24. Interestingly, scientists have discovered that   flies have a reproductive period from four hours to forty days depending upon the species. When pest controllers eradicate flies in a certain area, they spray pesticides every day for a forty day period. If they destroy the reproductive cycles of presently existing flies, they can kill off a whole generation of future flies.

Satan can't fight for long periods when he is resisted in Jesus' Name – he has to flee

The following stronghold busters are to help you pray through to breakthrough. Declare the prayers each day over your life.

At the end there is a list covering one to forty days. As you break the power of the lie over your life and declare God's truth you can tick off each of the forty days as you grow in victory.

The goal is not only to pull down ungodly, destructive strongholds, but to establish God's rule in their place.

The Apostle Paul says, *"Where the Spirit of the Lord is, there is freedom,"* 2 Corinthians 3:17. Therefore, being free is about learning how to allow the Spirit of Christ to rule and reign in our lives.

Freedom from Fear

*Fear is the darkroom where the devil
takes you to develop your negatives*

The Lie   There is nothing I can do to overcome my fears as I have lived with them too long.

I am just like my parents who lived in fear so maybe it's hereditary and I just have to cope the best I can.

Fear is just a part of who I am and I will always be like it.

The Effects   Living with the expectation that something bad is going to happen.

Being controlled and captive to whatever you fear. It steals your joy and robs your peace.

The Truth   *The Lord is my light and my salvation – whom shall I fear? The Lord is the stronghold of my life – of whom shall I be afraid? When evil men advance against me to devour my flesh, when my enemies and my foes attack me, they will stumble and fall. Though an army besiege me, my heart will not fear; though war break out against me, even then will I be confident.*

Psalm 27:1-3

I sought the Lord and He answered me and He delivered me from all my fears.

Psalm 34:4

But now, this is what the Lord says, He who created you, O Jacob, He who formed you, O Israel: 'Fear not, for I have redeemed you.'

Isaiah 43:1

For you did not receive a spirit that makes you a slave again to fear, but you received the Spirit of Sonship. And by him we cry, 'Abba, Father.'

Romans 8:15

For God did not give us a spirit of fear, but a spirit of power, of love and of self-discipline.

2 Timothy 1:6, 7

*Because God has said, 'Never will I leave you; never will I forsake you.' So we say with confidence, the Lord is my helper; I **will** not be* *afraid. What can man do to me?*

Hebrews 13:5,6

Perfect love drives out fear.

1 John 4:18

Prayer

Heavenly Father, you told me not to fear, for you are with me. You said you will strengthen me, help me and uphold me. You also said that no evil would befall me, neither would any disaster come near my dwelling because you have given your angels charge of me to keep me in all my ways, (Psalm 91:10-11).

You said that no weapon that is formed against me will prosper and that you will silence every tongue that rises against me in judgement because I am your servant, (Isaiah 54:17). You told me to cast all my cares on you because you care for me, (1Peter 5:7), and that your perfect love will drive away every fear from my life, (1John 4:18).

Father, these are your words and I thank you for bringing them to pass. I thank you that your love is from everlasting to everlasting and you drew me to you with your loving kindness, (Jeremiah 31:3). Your love is a love that will never let me go, (Romans 8:38,39).

Therefore I renounce and rebuke all fear from my life and receive your love and life in their place.

In Jesus' name, Amen.

Forty days of breakthrough – tick off each day

1	2	3	4	5	6	7	8	9
10	11	12	13	14	15	16	17	18
19	20	21	22	23	24	25	26	27
28	29	30	31	32	33	34	35	36
37	38	39	40					

If God is for us it doesn't matter

who is against us

2

Loneliness

*The biggest disease today is not leprosy
or tuberculosis but rather a feeling of
being unwanted, uncared for and
deserted by everybody.*

Mother Teresa

The Lie   That I am abandoned and rejected.

No one really cares about me.

I will always feel and be alone.

The Effects   Withdrawing from others.

Thinking people don't like me.

Frightened and scared.

The Truth   *Even though I walk through the valley of the shadow of death, I will fear no evil, for you are with me; your rod and your staff, they comfort me.*

Psalm 23:4

Be strong and courageous. Do not fear or be in dread of them, for it is the Lord your God who goes with you. He will not leave you or forsake you.

Deuteronomy 31:6

But now, this is what the Lord says – he who created you, O Jacob, he who formed you, O Israel: 'Fear not, for I have redeemed you; I have summoned you by name; you are mine. When you pass through the waters, I will be with you; and when you pass through the rivers, they will not sweep over you. When you walk through the fire, you will not be burned; the flames will not set you ablaze.'

Isaiah 43:1,2

'For I know the plans I have for you,' declares the Lord, 'plans to prosper you and not to harm you, plans to give you hope and a future.'

Jeremiah 29:11

For I am convinced that neither death nor life, neither angels nor demons, neither the present

154

nor the future, nor any powers, neither height nor depth, nor anything else in all creation, will be able to separate us from the love of God that is in Christ Jesus our Lord.

Romans 8:38-39

Prayer

Heavenly Father, I renounce the lie that I am abandoned and forgotten and will be left on my own. I announce the truth that you love me, that you have plans to give me a hope and a future and that absolutely nothing can separate me from your love. For you, Lord, created me and know everything about me and your love and presence comforts and  *sustains me. Therefore, I declare that loneliness and the fear of being alone will not rule over and control my life.*

In Jesus' name, Amen.

Forty days of breakthrough – tick off each day

1	2	3	4	5	6	7	8	9
10	11	12	13	14	15	16	17	18
19	20	21	22	23	24	25	26	27
28	29	30	31	32	33	34	35	36
37	38	39	40					

Jesus died forsaken so we would never have to be alone

Footholds and Strongholds

3

Bad Sleep and Dreams

*The average individual sleeps about
220,000 hours during his or her lifetime,
while only one in four people claims to
always get a good night's sleep*

The Lie	This is just part of life and I will have to put up with it.
	Things will probably get worse and there is no answer except more and more medication.
The Effects	Fearful of trying to go to sleep and sleeping.
	Exhaustion, anxiety, torment and confusion.
The Truth	*I lie down and sleep; I wake again, because the Lord sustains me.*

Psalm 3:5

157

I will lie down and sleep in peace, for you alone, O Lord, make me dwell in safety.

Psalm 4:8

Therefore let everyone who is godly pray to you while you may be found; surely when the mighty waters rise, they will not reach him. You are my hiding place; you will protect me from trouble and surround me with songs of deliverance.

Psalm 32:6-7

He who dwells in the shelter of the Most High will rest in the shadow of the Almighty. I will say of the Lord, 'He is my refuge and my fortress, my God, in whom I trust.'

You will not fear the terror of night, nor the arrow that flies by day, nor the pestilence that stalks in the darkness, nor the plague that destroys at midday.

A thousand may fall at your side, ten thousand at your right hand, but it will not come near you.

If you make the Most High your dwelling – even the Lord, who is my refuge, then no harm will befall you, no disaster will come near your tent.

For he will command his angels concerning you to guard you in all your ways.

Psalm 91:1,2,5,6,9,10,11

When you lie down, you will not be afraid; when you lie down, your sleep will be sweet. Have no fear of sudden disaster or of the ruin that overtakes the wicked, for the Lord will be your confidence and will keep your foot from being snared.

Proverbs 3:24-26

Jesus said, 'Come to me, all you who are weary and burdened, and I will give you rest.'

Matthew 11:28

Prayer

Heavenly Father, I thank you that you watch over me while I am awake and when I am asleep. Help me to rest and heal me and free me from the memories and dreams that confuse and torment me. Help me to still my busy and troubled mind as I fix my thoughts and turn my heart to you before I sleep. I choose to  *rest in you, knowing that your love will sustain me and your power will protect me. I speak to my soul and say 'be at peace and put your hope and trust in God'. Lord, I thank you for your presence and protection this day, and I will lie down and rest this night in your loving arms.*

In Jesus' name, Amen.

Forty days of breakthrough – tick off each day

1	2	3	4	5	6	7	8	9
10	11	12	13	14	15	16	17	18
19	20	21	22	23	24	25	26	27
28	29	30	31	32	33	34	35	36
37	38	39	40					

God gives to His beloved sleep.

Psalm 127:2

4

Bitterness and Unforgiveness

No matter how long you nurse a grudge,
it won't get better

The Lie   I can't forgive because what was done is so terrible.

If I forgive then they will just get away with it.

Feeling the way I am helps me to deal with it better.

The Effects   Anger and resentment that eats away inside us robbing our peace, destroying our joy and ruining our life.

We are kept a prisoner to what was done and those who did it.

Bitterness that effects our health and spreads into other areas and aspects of our lives.

The Truth When we forgive we are not saying that what was done or said does not matter, but we are sending those things out of our life and putting them into God's hands for Him to deal with. Those who have sinned against us will answer to God.

The word forgiveness means "to send away". If someone dumped their rubbish in our home we have a choice, we can either let it stay there and attract vermin and disease, or we can gather it up and dump it in the bin. If we don't want rubbish in our homes then why would we let it stay and fester in our hearts?

He has showed you, O man, what is good. And what does the Lord require of you? To act justly and to love mercy and to walk humbly with your God.

Micah 6:8

After Job had prayed for his friends, the Lord made him prosperous again and gave him twice as much as he had before.

Job 42:10

Then Peter came to Jesus and asked, 'Lord, how many times shall I forgive my brother when he sins against me? Up to seven times?' Jesus answered, 'I tell you, not seven times, but seventy-seven times.'

Matthew 18:21,22

While they were stoning him, Stephen prayed, 'Lord Jesus, receive my spirit.' Then he fell on his knees and cried out, 'Lord, do not hold this sin against them.'

Acts 7:59-60

Bear with each other and forgive whatever grievances you may have against one another. Forgive as the Lord forgave you.

Colossians 3:13

Prayer

Lord Jesus, you forgave me when I was still your enemy and your love has captured my heart. Therefore, I choose as an act of my will to forgive those who have acted like enemies towards me. I pray that your grace will also capture their hearts because I know that they have to answer to you for what they have said and done towards me and those I love. I

refuse to hold on to the sins and deeds that have been done against me and I send these out of my life and will not become bitter by harbouring them in my heart. I declare today I am free from what has been said and done, and free from those who did them. I choose to walk with you in grace and mercy. Amen.

Forty days of breakthrough – tick off each day

1	2	3	4	5	6	7	8	9
10	11	12	13	14	15	16	17	18
19	20	21	22	23	24	25	26	27
28	29	30	31	32	33	34	35	36
37	38	39	40					

A believer at war with his brother cannot be at peace with his Father

5

Bad and Sinful Habits

*A nail is driven out by another nail;
habit is overcome by habit.*
Latin Proverb

The Lie	This will not really harm me or others.
	I have tried to break it and failed and I will never be free.
	Others are doing the same and even worse why should I worry?
The Effects	Damaging our mental, emotional, physical and spiritual health.
	Living as a victim and feeling a failure.
	Being controlled by what is destructive.

The Truth *For sin shall not be your master.*

Romans 6:14

Through Christ Jesus the law of the Spirit of life set me free from the law of sin and death.

Romans 8:2

Submit yourselves, then, to God. Resist the devil, and he will flee from you.

James 4:7

It is for freedom that Christ has set us free. Stand firm, then, and do not let yourselves be burdened again by a yoke of slavery.

Galatians 5:1

But the fruit of the Spirit is love, joy, peace, patience, kindness, goodness, faithfulness, gentleness and self-control.

Galatians 5:22,23

The weapons we fight with are not the weapons of the world. On the contrary, they have divine power to demolish strongholds. We demolish arguments and every pretension that sets itself up against the knowledge of God, and we take captive every thought to make it obedient to Christ.

2 Corinthians 10:4,5

Prayer

Father, your word says that if I call on you, you will answer me, you will be with me in trouble and you will honour and deliver me. You said that the power of your Spirit will set me free from the vicious cycle of sin and death in my life. I choose life, your life over the power and consequences of every destructive habit in my life. I ask you that today and  *every day you will strengthen and empower me to make good choices so that I will experience good consequences. You have promised that no weapon formed against me will prosper and I declare that no bad habit will prevail within or have power over me. I thank you for delivering, empowering and setting me free through the power of your Word and Spirit. Amen.*

Forty days of breakthrough – tick off each day

1	2	3	4	5	6	7	8	9
10	11	12	13	14	15	16	17	18
19	20	21	22	23	24	25	26	27
28	29	30	31	32	33	34	35	36
37	38	39	40					

*The only hope of a decreasing self
is an increasing Christ.*

F.B. Meyer

Footholds and Strongholds

6

Depression and Despair

Life isn't always fair but God is always good

The Lie	Nobody cares and can help me.
	There is no way out or through.
	This will last forever and things will only get worse.
The Effects	Misery and torment.
	A loss of energy and purpose.
	Existing and surviving instead of living and enjoying life.

The Truth

Why are you downcast, O my soul? Why so disturbed within me? Put your hope in God, for I will yet praise him, my Saviour and my God

Psalm 42:5,6

I waited patiently for the Lord; he turned to me and heard my cry. He lifted me out of the slimy pit, out of the mud and mire; he set my feet on a rock and gave me a firm place to stand. He put a new song in my mouth, a hymn of praise to our God. Many will see and fear and put their trust in the Lord.

Psalm 41:1-3

Hear my cry, O God; listen to my prayer. From the ends of the earth I call to you, I call as my heart grows faint; lead me to the rock that is higher than I. For you have been my refuge, a strong tower against the foe. I long to dwell in your tent forever and take refuge in the shelter of your wings.

Psalm 61:1-4

'For I know the plans I have for you,' declares the Lord, 'plans to prosper you and not to harm you, plans to give you hope and a future.'

Jeremiah 29:11

Yet this I call to mind and therefore I have hope: Because of the Lord's great love we are not consumed, for his compassions never fail. They are new every morning; great is your faithfulness.

Lamentations 3:21-23

The thief comes only to steal and kill and destroy; I have come that they may have life, and have it to the full

John 10:10

If God is for us, who can be against us?

Romans 8:31

Prayer

Heavenly Father, I declare that my hope is in you. Therefore I do not, and will not, live under the power of depression and despair for I know these will pass because your love and faithfulness to me endures and will last forever. I take authority today over the spirit and stronghold of anxiety and dread and declare that whatever I face and however I feel since God is for me no  *weapon formed against me can prevail. I declare that the joy of the Lord is my strength and the grace of God is my peace. Jesus said He has come to give me life in all its fullness and today I choose life.*

In Jesus' name, Amen.

171

Forty days of breakthrough – tick off each day

1	2	3	4	5	6	7	8	9
10	11	12	13	14	15	16	17	18
19	20	21	22	23	24	25	26	27
28	29	30	31	32	33	34	35	36
37	38	39	40					

*There is no pit so deep that
God's love is not deeper still.*

Corrie ten Boom

7

Envy and Jealousy

*Envy takes the joy, happiness, and
contentment out of living.*

Billy Graham

While envy and jealousy are closely related they are not the
same thing. Envy is a longing to possess what another has
while jealousy is resentment of them for having it.

The Lie   If I had what they have I would be happier and
more content.

If I don't have it why should anyone else?

The Effects   You live your life comparing yourself and what you have with others.

You are upset about what you don't have instead of being able to enjoy and be thankful for what you do have.

When such jealousy captures the mind it corrupts the heart as it becomes consumed with competitiveness and criticism.

When you are continually jealous and envious of what the world has you are saying that Jesus is not enough.

The Truth   One of the most important tests of Christian character is our reaction to God's blessing upon another person's life. Do we resent it or rejoice over it?

God wants to bless you and what He gives is the best for us.

Do not be overawed when a man grows rich, when the splendour of his house increases; for he will take nothing with him when he dies, his splendour will not descend with him.

Psalm 49:16-17

A heart at peace gives life to the body, but envy rots the bones.

Proverbs 14:30

Envy and Jealousy

Anger is cruel and fury overwhelming, but who can stand before jealousy?

Proverbs 27:4

Love is patient, love is kind. It does not envy, it does not boast, it is not proud.

1 Corinthians 13:4

Do nothing out of selfish ambition or vain conceit, but in humility consider others better than yourselves.

Philippians 2:3

But if you harbour bitter envy and selfish ambition in your hearts, do not boast about it or deny the truth. Such 'wisdom' does not come down from heaven but is earthly, unspiritual, of the devil. For where you have envy and selfish ambition, there you find disorder and every evil practice.

James 3:14-16

Therefore, rid yourselves of all malice and all deceit, hypocrisy, envy, and slander of every kind. Like new-born babies, crave pure spiritual milk, so that by it you may grow up in your salvation.

1 Peter 2:1-2

Prayer

Lord Jesus, please help me to stop comparing myself with what others have, how they look and who they are. Help me to be grateful for what I have so I may be able to enjoy and be able to receive and experience more. Forgive me for selfish ambitions and for becoming angry and resentful because I want what I see others have. Instead of being jealous I choose to love and ask you to bless others and in place of being an envious person I pray you will make me a thankful person.

Amen.

Forty days of breakthrough – tick off each day

1	2	3	4	5	6	7	8	9
10	11	12	13	14	15	16	17	18
19	20	21	22	23	24	25	26	27
28	29	30	31	32	33	34	35	36
37	38	39	40					

People green with envy are ripe for trouble

The person who covets is always poor

8

Fear of Man

*If you are afraid of criticism
then you will never do anything*

The Lie   You will only be accepted if you do what other people want and expect of you.

You will only be liked and loved if you do what others want.

You will never amount to anyone worthwhile unless you always fit in and conform.

The Effects   Inferiority and intimidation.

Being controlled and manipulated.

Never becoming who you were meant to be because you are constantly being what others want you to be.

The Truth You are unique and special and have a call and destiny all of your own. You are to become all that you can be, not all of what others want you to be.

No one will be able to stand up against you all the days of your life. As I was with Moses, so I will be with you; I will never leave you nor forsake you. Be strong and courageous, because you will lead these people to inherit the land I swore to their forefathers to give them. Be strong and very courageous.

Joshua 1:5-7

Fear of man will prove to be a snare, but whoever trusts in the Lord is kept safe.

Proverbs 29:25

'Before I formed you in the womb I knew you, before you were born I set you apart; I appointed you as a prophet to the nations.' 'Ah, Sovereign Lord,' I said, 'I do not know how to speak; I am only a child.'

But the Lord said to me, 'Do not say, "I am only a child." You must go to everyone I send you to and say whatever I command you. Do not be afraid of them, for I am with you and will rescue you,' declares the Lord.

Jeremiah 1:5-8

Peter and the other apostles replied, 'We must obey God rather than men!'

Acts 5:29

We speak as men approved by God to be entrusted with the gospel. We are not trying to please men but God, who tests our hearts.

1 Thessalonians 2:4

For this reason I remind you to fan into flame the gift of God, which is in you through the laying on of my hands. For God did not give us a spirit of timidity, but a spirit of power, of love and of self-discipline.

2 Timothy 2:6-7

God has said, 'Never will I leave you; never will I forsake you.' We say with confidence, 'The Lord is my helper; I will not be afraid. What can man do to me?'

Hebrews 13:5-6

Prayer

Holy Spirit, help me each day to be led by you and not controlled by what others think of me or want from me. I forgive those who have intimidated and bullied me and say 'no more' in Jesus' name. I break every ungodly tie between myself and those people and refuse to be

179

dominated by their spirit. Heal me where I have been damaged and fill those areas with your Spirit.

In Jesus' name, Amen.

Forty days of breakthrough – tick off each day

1	2	3	4	5	6	7	8	9
10	11	12	13	14	15	16	17	18
19	20	21	22	23	24	25	26	27
28	29	30	31	32	33	34	35	36
37	38	39	40					

On some positions, cowardice asks the question, is it expedient? And then expedience comes along and asks the question, is it politic? Vanity asks the question, is it popular? Conscience asks the question, is it right?

Martin Luther King

9

Failure and Low Self Esteem

He who knows us the best is the One
who loves us the most

The Lie   I might as well admit that I am no use and will
never be any good.

People only like me for what I can do and
unless I am a success in everything I will
never be accepted and wanted.

I will never be a success and even when things
go right I live in the fear that they will soon go
wrong.

The Effects   Anxiety and depression.

Learning to live at a very low level of faith and expectancy.

Feeling you have to be perfect to be loved and accepted.

The Truth   *For you created my inmost being; you knit me together in my mother's womb. I praise you because I am fearfully and wonderfully made.*

Psalm 139:13,14

'For I know the plans I have for you,' declares the Lord, 'plans to prosper you and not to harm you, plans to give you hope and a future.'

Jeremiah 29:11

I have loved you with an everlasting love; I have drawn you with loving-kindness. I will build you up again and you will be rebuilt.

Jeremiah 31:4,5

Yet this I call to mind and therefore I have hope: Because of the Lord's great love we are not consumed, for his compassions never fail. They are new every morning; great is your faithfulness.

Lamentations 3:21-23

Therefore, there is now no condemnation for those who are in Christ Jesus.

Romans 8:1

And by him we cry, 'Abba, Father.' The Spirit testifies with our spirit that we are God's children.

Romans 8:15-16

For I am convinced that neither death nor life, neither angels nor demons, neither the present nor the future, nor any powers, neither height nor depth, nor anything else in all creation, will be able to separate us from the love of God that is in Christ Jesus our Lord.

Romans 8:38-39

I can do everything through him (Christ) who gives me strength.

Philippians 4:13

Prayer

Lord Jesus, I give to you the pain of all my disappointments. I realise that even though there are times I may fail I can never be a failure because you have chosen me and love me and I am your child. I receive healing through your Holy Spirit as I give you the broken pieces of my fears and failures. I receive your strength and

183

wholeness. I will be still and know that you are God and know how special and significant I am because of whose I am. I will not live in the grip of failure because you have engraved me on the palms of your hands and because you are with me and for me I not will fret over what may come against me. You have chosen me with graciousness and called me to greatness.

Amen.

Forty days of breakthrough – tick off each day

1	2	3	4	5	6	7	8	9
10	11	12	13	14	15	16	17	18
19	20	21	22	23	24	25	26	27
28	29	30	31	32	33	34	35	36
37	38	39	40					

*God loves every one of us as if there were
but one of us to love.*

St Augustine

10

Freedom from the Fear of the Devil

If God is for us it doesn't matter who is against us

The Lie Demonic powers are so strong they can attack and overcome you any time they want to.

If you go on the front line of the battle for God then you are going to be targeted by the enemy and will be oppressed and defeated.

Living in the fear of the devil and demonic powers.

The Effects   Living life on the defensive.

Fearful of stepping out for God.

Living under oppression and anxiety.

The Truth   Only God is all powerful, everywhere present and knowing everything. The devil and his demons are powerful but limited, they do not know everything and the devil cannot be everywhere. They have to submit to the authority God's people have in Jesus' name.

He who dwells in the shelter of the Most High will rest in the shadow of the Almighty. I will say of the Lord, 'He is my refuge and my fortress, my God, in whom I trust.' Surely he will save you from the fowler's snare and from the deadly pestilence. He will cover you with his feathers, and under his wings you will find refuge; his faithfulness will be your shield and rampart. You will not fear the terror of night, nor the arrow that flies by day, nor the pestilence that stalks in the darkness, nor the plague that destroys at midday.

A thousand may fall at your side, ten thousand at your right hand, but it will not come near you.

Psalm 91:1-7

No weapon forged against you will prevail.

Isaiah 54:17

I have given you authority to trample on snakes and scorpions and to overcome all the power of the enemy; nothing will harm you.

Luke 10:19

If God is for us, who can be against us?

Romans 8:31

Submit yourselves, then, to God. Resist the devil, and he will flee from you.

James 4:7

They overcame him (the devil) by the blood of the Lamb and by the word of their testimony.

Revelation 12:11

Greater is He that is in us than he (the devil) that is in the world.

1 John 4:4

Prayer

Heavenly Father, your will for my life is that I live in freedom and faith – not fear and bondage. You are almighty, all knowing and everywhere present and there is no person or power that can compare with you. Lord Jesus, on the cross you defeated the devil and all his demons and made a public

187

spectacle of them. Therefore, in you I am completely victorious over every demonic power. When I submit to your will and your love and resist the devil he has to flee from me. Even if I walk through the darkest valley I will fear no evil because you have promised to be with me and always bring me through victorious.

Amen.

Forty days of breakthrough – tick off each day

1	2	3	4	5	6	7	8	9
10	11	12	13	14	15	16	17	18
19	20	21	22	23	24	25	26	27
28	29	30	31	32	33	34	35	36
37	38	39	40					

He who kneels before God can
stand before anyone

11

Condemnation and Guilt

1 cross + 3 nails = 4 given

The Lie
You are just a miserable sinner and failure.

You won't and don't deserve to be forgiven.

You have committed the unforgiveable sin.

The Effects
Constantly replaying what you have done wrong and beating yourself up over it.

Torment and despair robbing you of your joy and peace.

Living in defeat and feeling like giving up.

The Truth   Jesus who knows you best is also the one who loves you most. It is the devil who condemns you for he is the accuser of God's people. The Holy Spirit will convict you because He wants you restored and cleansed.

The unforgivable sin is blasphemy against the Holy Spirit which means that your heart has become so hardened you would rather side with the devil than God and refuse to repent over your sins.

Cleanse me with hyssop, and I will be clean; wash me, and I will be whiter than snow… Create in me a pure heart, O God, and renew a steadfast spirit within me. Do not cast me from your presence or take your Holy Spirit from me. Restore to me the joy of your salvation and grant me a willing spirit, to sustain me.

Psalm 51:7-12

I, even I, am he who blots out your transgressions, for my own sake, and remembers your sins no more.

Isaiah 43:25

You will again have compassion on us; you will tread our sins underfoot and hurl all our iniquities into the depths of the sea.

Micah 7:19

The Lord is compassionate and gracious, slow to anger, abounding in love. He will not always accuse, nor will he harbour his anger forever; he does not treat us as our sins deserve or repay us according to our iniquities. For as high as the heavens are above the earth, so great is his love for those who fear him; as far as the east is from the west, so far has he removed our transgressions from us. As a father has compassion on his children, so the Lord has compassion on those who fear him.

Psalm 103:8-13

Therefore, there is now no condemnation for those who are in Christ Jesus, because through Christ Jesus the law of the Spirit of life set me free from the law of sin and death.

Romans 8:1,2

For I will forgive their wickedness and will remember their sins no more.

Hebrews 8:12

If we confess our sins, he is faithful and just and will forgive us our sins and purify us from all unrighteousness.

1 John 1:9

Prayer

Lord Jesus, I confess my sin before you asking for and receiving forgiveness through your blood that was shed for me. Your Word tells me that if I confess my sin you are faithful and just and will forgive me and cleanse me from all unrighteousness. Therefore, I declare over my life and in my  *heart today that I am forgiven because I have repented and on the cross you took and paid the price for all my sin. I take my stand and every time the enemy seeks to remind me of my sin and failure it will drive me to you and not from you. I therefore rebuke in the name of Jesus every spirit of condemnation and accusation that has come against me. I am a new creation, no more in condemnation and in the grace of God I stand. Amen.*

Forty days of breakthrough – tick off each day

1	2	3	4	5	6	7	8	9
10	11	12	13	14	15	16	17	18
19	20	21	22	23	24	25	26	27
28	29	30	31	32	33	34	35	36
37	38	39	40					

When the Lord takes your sins you never see them again. He casts them into the depths of the sea, forgiven and forgotten. I even believe he places a sign over them that reads, 'No fishing allowed.'

Corrie ten Boom

Greed and the Love of Money

The Jews have a saying,
'Whosoever craves wealth is like a man who drinks sea water.
The more he drinks the more he thirsts and he ceases
not to drink until he perishes.'

The Lie	Happiness and security are found in money so the more money I have the happier and more secure I will be.
	Money has the power to give me everything I need.
The Effects	When money has power and control over my life it corrupts and compromises my values and my virtues.
	Greed deceives and destroys.

The Truth   The Bible does not say money is the root of all evil but rather *'the love of money is the root of all kinds of evil'*. Money itself is neutral, it can be used for good and bad, but when we start to love it and it becomes our pursuit and passion it has the capacity to take us captive and instead of a servant it becomes a master, instead of an income for working it becomes an idol for worshipping.

Whoever loves money never has money enough; whoever loves wealth is never satisfied with his income.

Ecclesiastes 5:10

Come, all you who are thirsty, come to the waters; and you who have no money, come, buy and eat! Come, buy wine and milk without money and without cost. Why spend money on what is not bread, and your labour on what does not satisfy? Listen, listen to me, and eat what is good, and your soul will delight in the richest of fare.

Isaiah 55:1,2

No one can serve two masters. Either he will hate the one and love the other, or he will be devoted to the one and despise the other. You cannot serve both God and money.

Matthew 6:24

The one who received the seed that fell among the thorns is the man who hears the word, but the worries of this life and the deceitfulness of wealth choke it, making it unfruitful.

Matthew 13:22

Then he said to them, 'Watch out! Be on your guard against all kinds of greed; a man's life does not consist in the abundance of his possessions.'

And he told them this parable: 'The ground of a certain rich man produced a good crop. He thought to himself, "What shall I do? I have no place to store my crops." Then he said, "This is what I'll do. I will tear down my barns and build bigger ones, and there I will store all my grain and my goods. And I'll say to myself, 'You have plenty of good things laid up for many years. Take life easy; eat, drink and be merry.'" But God said to him, "You fool! This very night your life will be demanded from you. Then who will get what you have prepared for yourself?" This is how it will be with anyone who stores up things for himself but is not rich toward God.'

Luke 12:15-21

For the love of money is a root of all kinds of evil. Some people, eager for money, have wandered from the faith and pierced themselves with many griefs.

1 Timothy 6:10

Keep your lives free from the love of money and be content with what you have, because God has said, 'Never will I leave you; never will I forsake you.' So we say with confidence, 'The Lord is my helper; I will not be afraid. What can man do to me?'

Hebrews 3:5,6

Prayer

Lord Jesus, I repent of my love of money and the power it has over my life. I renounce greed and all cravings for this world's wealth. I look to you for my provision and security and ask that you make me a good steward so I can be trusted with more of what you desire to bless me with both spiritually and financially. My desire is to live with power over money and greed and not for  *them to have power over me. Come and rule and reign in my heart for you are the greatest treasure that I seek. Amen.*

Forty days of breakthrough – tick off each day

1	2	3	4	5	6	7	8	9
10	11	12	13	14	15	16	17	18
19	20	21	22	23	24	25	26	27
28	29	30	31	32	33	34	35	36
37	38	39	40					

Give God what's right not what's left

13

Lust and Sexual Sin

*Forbidden fruits create
many jams*

The Lie   I am in control of my lust and it fulfils me.

Everyone else seems to be the same so I would be strange if I was any different.

I am the master of my desires and something that feels so pleasurable cannot be so wrong.

The Effects   Instead of you having healthy and godly sexual desires, ungodly ones take you captive.

Desires and lusts become increasingly stronger and need ever increasing satisfaction.

People become objects instead of persons.

The Truth   We are made to love and for love, but lust is about having to satisfy yourself with no or little concern about how you do it. Lust and ungodly sexual sin is not freedom – it always leads to deeper and deeper bondage.

Create in me a pure heart, O God, and renew a steadfast spirit within me. Do not cast me from your presence or take your Holy Spirit from me. Restore to me the joy of your salvation and grant me a willing spirit, to sustain me.

Psalm 51:10-12

How can a young man keep his way pure? By living according to your word. I seek you with all my heart; do not let me stray from your commands. I have hidden your word in my heart that I might not sin against you.

Psalm 119:9-11

For sin shall not be your master, because you are not under law, but under grace.

Romans 6:14

Since, then, you have been raised with Christ, set your hearts on things above, where Christ is seated at the right hand of God. Set your minds on things above, not on earthly things.

Colossians 3:1,2

When tempted, no one should say, 'God is tempting me.' For God cannot be tempted by evil, nor does he tempt anyone; but each one is tempted when, by his own evil desire, he is dragged away and enticed. Then, after desire has conceived, it gives birth to sin; and sin, when it is full-grown, gives birth to death. If we claim to be without sin, we deceive ourselves and the truth is not in us.

James 1:13-15

If we confess our sins, he is faithful and just and will forgive us our sins and purify us from all unrighteousness.

1 John 1:8-9

Prayer

Heavenly Father, you know the struggles that I have and my longing to be free from sexual sin and the power of lust. I call on you today to heal me and deliver me and give me strength to stand against and overcome the power of these things in my life. I will keep short accounts with  *you and if I slip I will not sink and I will not let a spill become a stain for I choose to walk in the light and not fool myself that I am doing no wrong. Create in me a clean heart and renew in me a right spirit that I will live in victory. Help me to hide your word in my heart so I will not sin against you but by your grace will keep my ways pure.*

In Jesus' name. Amen.

Forty days of breakthrough – tick off each day

1	2	3	4	5	6	7	8	9
10	11	12	13	14	15	16	17	18
19	20	21	22	23	24	25	26	27
28	29	30	31	32	33	34	35	36
37	38	39	40					

*David's pleasure with Bathsheba
caused him to lose his joy.*

Psalm 51:11

14

Pornography

I made a covenant with my eyes not to look lustfully at a young woman.

Job 31:1

The Lie   Pornography will bring lasting pleasure and joy and it will not harm me.

Pornography doesn't really hurt anyone.

The Effects   Shame, warped sexual feelings, unable to relate to other people as God intended, harmful to my marriage and other relationships.

The Truth   *Jesus said, 'I tell you that anyone who looks at a woman lustfully has already committed adultery with her in his heart.'*

Matthew 5:28

In the same way, count yourselves dead to sin but alive to God in Christ Jesus. Therefore do not let sin reign in your mortal body so that you obey its evil desires. Do not offer the parts of your body to sin, as instruments of wickedness, but rather offer yourselves to God, as those who have been brought from death to life; and offer the parts of your body to him as instruments of righteousness. For sin shall not be your master, because you are not under law, but under grace.

Romans 6:11-14

Do you not know that your body is a temple of the Holy Spirit?

1 Corinthians 6:19

No temptation has seized you except what is common to man. And God is faithful; he will not let you be tempted beyond what you can bear. But when you are tempted, he will also provide a way out so that you can stand up under it.

1 Corinthians 10:13

So I say, live by the Spirit and you will not gratify the desires of the flesh.

Galatians 5:16

But the fruit of the Spirit is love, joy, peace, patience, kindness, goodness, faithfulness, gentleness and self-control. Against such things there is no law. Those who belong to Christ Jesus have crucified the flesh with its passions and desires.

Galatians 5:22

Prayer

Heavenly Father, I renounce the lie that I cannot resist the temptation to look at pornography. I declare the truth that God will always provide a way out when I am tempted and I will choose to take it. I announce the truth that if I live by the Spirit – and I choose to do that – I will not gratify the desires of the flesh and that the fruit of the Spirit, including self-control,  *will grow in me. I count myself dead to sin and refuse to let sin reign in my body or be my master. Today and every day I give my body to God as a temple of the Holy Spirit to be used only for what is right. I declare that the power of sin is broken in me. I choose to submit completely to God and resist the devil who must flee.*

In Jesus' name. Amen.

Forty days of breakthrough – tick off each day

1	2	3	4	5	6	7	8	9
10	11	12	13	14	15	16	17	18
19	20	21	22	23	24	25	26	27
28	29	30	31	32	33	34	35	36
37	38	39	40					

Every pornographic image
is someone's child

15

Suicidal Thoughts

Suicide is not the answer... Jesus is

The Lie   I would be better off dead.

Others would be better off without me.

There is no way things are going to get better.

Death is the best way out.

The Effects   Opening your life to the spirit of death which not only wants to destroy the quantity but also the quality of your life.

Depression and anxiety become a constant companion.

Everything becomes negative.

The Truth God has created you for a purpose and His will is that you experience life in all its fullness as you live it with Him. Suicide and harming your life is not the answer – Jesus is.

But I trust in you, O Lord; I say, 'You are my God.' My times are in your hands; deliver me from my enemies and from those who pursue me. Let your face shine on your servant; save me in your unfailing love.

Psalm 31:14-16

In God I trust; I will not be afraid. What can man do to me? For you have delivered me from death and my feet from stumbling, that I may walk before God in the light of life.

Psalm 56:11,13

'For I know the plans I have for you,' declares the Lord, 'plans to prosper you and not to harm you, plans to give you hope and a future.'

Jeremiah 29:11

Come to me, all you who are weary and burdened, and I will give you rest. Take my yoke upon you and learn from me, for I am gentle and humble in heart, and you will find rest for your souls.

Matthew 11:28,29

The thief comes only to steal and kill and destroy; I have come that they may have life, and have it to the full.

John 10:10

Cast all your anxiety on him because he cares for you.

1 Peter 5:7

Prayer

Jesus, my heart is heavy and my mind is troubled and confused. I do not know where to turn or what to do. Therefore, I call to you in my pain and my distress. For you know what anguish and despair feels like because you hung upon a cross and were forsaken. But you rose from the dead and conquered death and in your name and through your love and power I also have

victory over the thoughts of death that play on my mind and torment me. I know that you are the answer and not suicide, and therefore I repent of and renounce every agreement I have made with suicide to find comfort or peace. I rebuke every spirit of death that taunts and tempts me and I choose life for your will and plans for me are good and my hope is in you. Today is the day that you have made and I ask for your strength to rejoice in it and rest in you.

Amen.

Forty days of breakthrough – tick off each day

1	2	3	4	5	6	7	8	9
10	11	12	13	14	15	16	17	18
19	20	21	22	23	24	25	26	27
28	29	30	31	32	33	34	35	36
37	38	39	40					

Jesus not only gives life, He gives
the power to enjoy life

16

Fear of Sickness and Death

*Jesus died to give His life for us and
rose again to give His life to us*

The Lie   I will become sick and die of the same illness as my parents or others I know.

As I grow older sickness will fill my life.

The Effects   Fearful and anxious about sickness and dying.

Imagining one illness after another.

Living in torment of having cancer or some other disease.

Constantly imagining the worst.

The Truth

The Lord is my light and my salvation, whom shall I fear? The Lord is the stronghold of my life – of whom shall I be afraid?

Psalm 27:1

Surely he will save you from the fowler's snare and from the deadly pestilence. He will cover you with his feathers, and under his wings you will find refuge; his faithfulness will be your shield and rampart. You will not fear the terror of night, nor the arrow that flies by day, nor the pestilence that stalks in the darkness, nor the plague that destroys at midday.

Psalm 91:3-6

If you make the Most High your dwelling – even the Lord, who is my refuge, then no harm will befall you, no disaster will come near your tent. For he will command his angels concerning you to guard you in all your ways.

Psalm 91:9-11

'Because he loves me,' says the Lord, 'I will rescue him; I will protect him, for he acknowledges my name. He will call upon me, and I will answer him; I will be with him in trouble, I will deliver him and honour him. With long life will I satisfy him and show him my salvation.'

Psalm 91:14-16

Do not be afraid. I am the First and the Last. I am the Living One; I was dead, and behold I am alive for ever and ever! And I hold the keys of death and Hades.

Revelation 1:17,18

All the days ordained for me were written in your book before one of them came to be.

Psalm 139:16

I am the God who heals you.

Exodus 15:26

Prayer

In you, Lord Jesus, death and sickness have no power over me and no authority in my life. Therefore, I break the power of the fear of death and disease in the name of Jesus who is the resurrection and the life. I take authority this day over every anxiety of becoming unwell. I declare in you, Lord Jesus, I am saved from death's powers not only when I die but also as I  *live. Therefore, today I choose life and to focus on health and wellbeing. Jesus, I thank you that you took up my infirmities and have carried all my diseases.*

Amen.

Forty days of breakthrough – tick off each day

1	2	3	4	5	6	7	8	9
10	11	12	13	14	15	16	17	18
19	20	21	22	23	24	25	26	27
28	29	30	31	32	33	34	35	36
37	38	39	40					

Our lives are hid with Christ in God.

Colossians 3:3

17

Pride and Prejudice

God sends no one away empty except those who are full of themselves

D.L. Moody

The Lie   I am my own master and will control my own destiny.

I am superior therefore I can look down on others.

The Effects   Selfishness and personal ambition control your life.

You may rise to great heights but you will also have great falls.

Arrogance and indifference capture your heart and you demean and devalue others.

The Truth   In the world greatness is measured by how many serve you, but in the Kingdom of God greatness is measured by how many you serve. We can never develop a servant heart when it is mastered by pride and prejudice.

But after Uzziah became powerful, his pride led to his downfall. He was unfaithful to the Lord his God.

2 Chronicles 26:16

When pride comes, then comes disgrace, but with humility comes wisdom.

Proverbs 11:2

Pride only breeds quarrels, but wisdom is found in those who take advice.

Proverbs 13:10

Pride goes before destruction, a haughty spirit before a fall.

Proverbs 16:18

Love is patient, love is kind. It does not envy, it does not boast, it is not proud.

1 Corinthians 13:4

Prayer

Heavenly Father, I confess my sinful and proud attitudes and behaviour. Forgive me for my prejudices and the way I feel superior to others and look down upon them. Help me to see people and love them the way you see and love them. Help me to walk in humility so I can walk with you.

In Jesus' name, Amen.

Forty days of breakthrough – tick off each day

1	2	3	4	5	6	7	8	9
10	11	12	13	14	15	16	17	18
19	20	21	22	23	24	25	26	27
28	29	30	31	32	33	34	35	36
37	38	39	40					

When a man is wrapped up in himself he makes a pretty small package.

John Ruskin

18

Comfort in
Food and Not in God

*We will find more comfort in God's compassion
than in a million calories*

The Lie   Food and overeating brings lasting comfort.

                  The more I eat the better I will be.

                  I can solve my problems with eating.

The Effect   Harmful to health.

                  Food becoming an idol.

                  A form of substance abuse.

The Truth   *Like a city whose walls are broken down is a man who lacks self-control.*

Proverbs 25:28

So I say, live by the Spirit, and you will not gratify the desires of the flesh.

Galatians 5:16

But the fruit of the Spirit is love, joy, peace, patience, kindness, goodness, faithfulness, gentleness and self-control.

Galatians 5:22

Praise be to the God and Father of our Lord Jesus Christ, the Father of compassion and the God of all comfort, who comforts us in all our troubles, so that we can comfort those in any trouble with the comfort we ourselves have received from God.

2 Corinthians 1:3-4

I will praise you as long as I live, and in your name I will lift up my hands. My soul will be satisfied as with the richest of foods; with singing lips my mouth will praise you.

Psalm 63:4-5

May your unfailing love be my comfort, according to your promise to your servant.

Psalm 119:76

Prayer

Heavenly Father, I renounce the lie that food and overeating brings lasting comfort. I announce the truth that you are the God of all comfort and that your unfailing love is my only legitimate and real comfort. I affirm that I now live by the Spirit and do not have to gratify the desires of the flesh. Whenever I feel in need of comfort, instead of turning to foods I choose to praise you and be satisfied as with the richest of foods. Fill me afresh with your Holy Spirit and live through me as I grow in self-control.

In Jesus' name, Amen.

Forty days of breakthrough – tick off each day

1	2	3	4	5	6	7	8	9
10	11	12	13	14	15	16	17	18
19	20	21	22	23	24	25	26	27
28	29	30	31	32	33	34	35	36
37	38	39	40					

When it comes to eating, you can sometimes help yourself more by helping yourself less

Ungodly Anger and Rage

When the only tool you have is a hammer
you tend to see every problem as a nail

The Lie   I cannot help the way I am.

                     People deserve it when I lose my temper.

The Effects   Internal tension and stress.

                     Alienating and harming others.

                     Violence and depression.

The Truth

Then the Lord said to Cain, 'Why are you angry? Why is your face downcast? If you do what is right, will you not be accepted? But if you do not do what is right, sin is crouching at your door; it desires to have you, but you must master it.'

Genesis 4:6,8

Refrain from anger and turn from wrath; do not fret – it leads only to evil.

Psalm 37:8

A gentle answer turns away wrath, but a harsh word stirs up anger.

Proverbs 15:1

Better a patient man than a warrior, a man who controls his temper than one who takes a city.

Proverbs 16:32

Do not take revenge, my friends, but leave room for God's wrath, for it is written: 'It is mine to avenge; I will repay,' says the Lord. On the contrary: 'If your enemy is hungry, feed him; if he is thirsty, give him something to drink. In doing this, you will heap burning coals on his head.' Do not be overcome by evil, but overcome evil with good.

Romans 12:19-21

*But the fruit of the Spirit is love, joy, peace,
patience, kindness, goodness, faithfulness,
gentleness and self-control.*

Galatians 5:22-23

Prayer

*Lord, forgive me for my ungodly anger and
bad temper. Help me to respond to
circumstances and people in love and
wisdom and not in fury and rage. Heal my
heart and emotions so I do not strike out
against others and help me to control my
tongue and what I say and the way I say it.
Forgive me if I have used my anger and*

*temper to try and control others and help me today to control
myself. Give me the strength to have mercy and forgive, Amen.*

Forty days of breakthrough – tick off each day

1	2	3	4	5	6	7	8	9
10	11	12	13	14	15	16	17	18
19	20	21	22	23	24	25	26	27
28	29	30	31	32	33	34	35	36
37	38	39	40					

*When something happens to make you feel angry or
hurt, instead of saying 'why did they do that?' ask first
'why am I feeling and reacting like this?'*

20

Anxiety and Worry

Worry gives a small thing a big shadow

The Lie   Something bad is bound to happen.

Things will get worst and go wrong.

This will never end.

The Effects   Depression and sickness.

Fearful and living on the edge.

Tired and weary of life.

The Truth   *From the ends of the earth I call to you, I call as my heart grows faint; lead me to the rock that is higher than I. For you have been my refuge, a strong tower against the foe.*

Psalm 61:2,3

Trust in the Lord with all your heart, and do not lean on your own understanding. In all your ways acknowledge him, and he will make straight your paths.

Proverbs 3:5-6

Fear not, for I am with you; be not dismayed, for I am your God; I will strengthen you, I will help you, I will uphold you with my righteous right hand.

Isaiah 41:10

Humble yourselves, therefore, under the mighty hand of God so that at the proper time he may exalt you, casting all your anxieties on him, because he cares for you.

1 Peter 5:6,7

Do not be anxious about anything, but in everything by prayer and supplication with thanksgiving let your requests be made known to God. And the peace of God, which surpasses all understanding, will guard your hearts and your minds in Christ Jesus.

Philippians 4:6-7

God has said, 'Never will I leave you or forsake you.'

Hebrews 13:5

Prayer

Heavenly Father, You are my peace.
Therefore, no matter what the
circumstances I do not have to fear and
will not live in worry and anxiety. I thank
you that there is nothing that can happen in
my life that will ever take you by surprise
or is bigger than you. Every anxious issue
within me I give to you right now and in its

place I receive your love and peace. You have promised to
meet all my needs and I declare your Lordship over every care
and concern I have and will ever have. In Jesus' Name, Amen.

Forty days of breakthrough – tick off each day

1	2	3	4	5	6	7	8	9
10	11	12	13	14	15	16	17	18
19	20	21	22	23	24	25	26	27
28	29	30	31	32	33	34	35	36
37	38	39	40					

Worry is like a rocking chair, it will give you
something to do, but it won't get you anywhere.

21

Rejection

*God loves each one of us as if there was
only one of us to love.*

St. Augustine

The Lie   I am not wanted and will never be wanted.

I will never be loved.

There must be something wrong with me.

The Effects   Loneliness and low self worth.

Fearful and apprehensive.

Unable to form meaningful friendships
and relationships.

The Truth

The Lord is close to the brokenhearted and saves those who are crushed in spirit.

Psalm 34:18

The Lord appeared to us in the past, saying: "I have loved you with an everlasting love; I have drawn you with unfailing kindness.

Jeremiah 31:3

All that the Father gives me will come to me, and whoever comes to me I will never drive away.

John 6:37

For he chose us in him before the creation of the world to be holy and blameless in his sight.

Ephesians 1:4

God has said, "Never will I leave you; never will I forsake you." So we say with confidence, "The Lord is my helper; I will not be afraid. What can man do to me?"

Hebrews 13:5,6

Prayer

In the name of Jesus, I renounce every spirit of rejection, fear of rejection, self rejection, and perceived rejection that has ever entered and become a part of my life.

I close every door against rejection and cancel every legal right that rejection has had to operate in my life. I declare that I am loved by God who has said He will never leave me or forsake me. He will never reject me or abandon me. I declare that by God's grace I will not live in the fear of rejection but will make healthy and loving relationships.

I am loved and I will love in Jesus' Name. Amen

Forty days of breakthrough – tick off each day

1	2	3	4	5	6	7	8	9
10	11	12	13	14	15	16	17	18
19	20	21	22	23	24	25	26	27
28	29	30	31	32	33	34	35	36
37	38	39	40					

Two children were arguing about their parents' love. The first child said, "My mummy and daddy love me more that yours love you because I am their child while yours only adopted you." "That's true," said the other child, "but my mummy and daddy chose me while yours had no choice."

Appendix 1

The Three Stages of Bondage

The Spirit of the Sovereign Lord is upon me, because the Lord has anointed me to preach good news to the poor. He has sent me to bind up the brokenhearted, to proclaim freedom for the captives and release from darkness for the prisoners.

Isaiah 61:1

In Matthew 8:16-17, it tells us how Jesus fulfilled the prophecy of Him taking on our iniquities/infirmities and it is in the context of Him healing the sick and casting out demons.

Captives and Prisoners

It is helpful to note that Isaiah distinguishes between two types of people who are bound; one he calls *captives* and the other he refers to as *prisoners*. Whilst it is important that we don't make too much of this it is useful in helping us understand that there are different types and degrees of bondage.

When ministering to set someone free who is demonised, understanding whether they are a prisoner or a captive can help us know the best way to proceed.

Prisoners are usually criminals whom a judge has sent to jail because of their own wrong doing, (Matthew 18:21-35).

Captives, however, are people imprisoned because of what others have done to them and the lies and deception they have believed.

The Bible makes it clear that there are different kinds of demons that cause problems to people. Some demons cause blindness, others cause deafness, others mental illness, others cause fear and depression (King Saul), others epilepsy (Matthew 17:15-21), and so forth. Therefore, if a person is under the power of a spirit of blindness, they won't see (Matthew 12:22), if they are under the power of a spirit of infirmity, they will have some sort of physical ailment (Luke 13:11), if they are under the power of a spirit of fear, they will be fearful, or if they are under the power of a spirit of anger, they will have problems with anger.

Either the demon(s) was there before the person came to Christ (past lifestyle, generational curse, bondages they previously came under, vows they made with the enemy, etc), or after they became a Christian. The way demons gain access into a believer's life is through open doors.

There are certain sins we can do that will defile us (make us unclean). For example, having unholy sex can create ungodly soul ties which serve as demonic bridges and can pass bondages from one person to another.

Either way, the open door (if any) needs to be shut, and the demons cast out. Just because the enemy may lose legal rights to stay in someone's life through the person repenting, it doesn't mean he always leaves immediately. Even though Jesus paid the price for our iniquities (Isaiah 53:5), it doesn't mean the demons won't want to hang around until they are actually kicked out. If demons always left automatically when their rights were removed and immediately after we are saved then there would be no need to cast them out.

The dangers of casting a demon out of a non-believer

"When an impure spirit comes out of a person, it goes through arid places seeking rest and does not find it. Then it says, 'I will return to the house I left.' When it arrives, it finds the house unoccupied, swept clean and put in order. Then it goes and takes with it seven other spirits more wicked than itself, and they go in and live there. And the final condition of that person is worse than the first. That is how it will be with this wicked generation." Matthew 12:43-45.

Trying to cast a demon out of an unbeliever is not a wise idea unless that person is possessed and needs first to be set free before they can make a decision to follow Jesus. Therefore when possible it is always wise to first lead the person to Jesus and then minister deliverance.

Prayer and Fasting

Jesus said, *"**This kind** can come out by nothing but prayer and fasting,"* Mark 9:29.

Some demonic spirits are more powerful than others and have a greater hold on a person's life. Jesus is saying that it requires more faith and authority to cast these demons out and this only comes by spending time with God and seeking Him earnestly.

Three Stages of Bondage

Stage one: Ignorance and deception

Jesus said, *"You will know the truth and the truth will set you free,"* John 8:32. Ignorance and believing the devil's lies will not only take you captive they will keep you bound. Breaking this kind of bondage is exposing the power of the lie and establishing the truth of God's Word in a person's life.

Stage two: When sin has given the devil a legal right

These kind of bondages have a root in either sin the person has committed or sin that has been committed against them. The enemy's legal rights must be broken and taken away, therefore repentance and forgiveness are at the heart of such deliverance.

Stage three: Demonic powers must be driven out

Stages one and two usually involve demonic forces being driven from and off a person and many times that is usually sufficient. However, such powers can also infect and invade a person's life so that they must be *driven* out from them.

Scars into Stars

There was a lady in a church I pastored who had been terribly abused as a child. Traumatised and brutalised by her experiences she became a prostitute in later life. Naturally it seems a strange choice knowing what she went through but all she had known was abuse by men and so the pain and powers within her drove her to know more.

To cut a very long story short she was wonderful saved. She sat in the front row of the church and was always one of the first to raise her hands and arms to worship God. What was so significant is that her arms had chunks of flesh that she had cut out of them when she used to self harm to medicate her pain. But now she raised them up in praise to God who had truly healed her and set her free.

Footholds and Strongholds

Appendix 2

Can a Christian Have a Demon?

Before wc answer that "explosive" issue let's ask ourselves some other questions.

Can a Christian have a sickness and disease?

Can a Christian have a destructive bondage and addiction?

Can a Christian commit sin?

Can a Christian commit adultery?

Can a Christian be deceived?

Can a Christian have a problem with anger and rage?

Can a Christian have an unteachable and bitter spirit?

While your answers to these questions don't automatically answer whether or not a Christian can have a demon, they do at least help us to understand that a Christian can have and be influenced and controlled by a great deal that is ungodly and evil.

The reason for this is that God's forgiveness and righteousness in salvation is first imputed (credited to us in Christ) and then begins the process of His righteousness being imparted to us. The first we call *justification* and then comes *sanctification* as we yield to God and His Holy Spirit to make us more Christ like.

It is also important to realise that when talking about the spiritual realm our understanding tends to be limited to the natural laws and language of the visible world. We tend to explain spiritual realities with precise and neat definitions, even while arguing over the meaning of specific words in the original language. This may help us to feel intelligent and informed, yet the spirit world will not stay in these well defined boxes.

Anyone who has ever experienced the demonic or angelic realm will tell you that our vocabulary is insufficient to describe the realities of this dimension. For example, we have principles like the laws of physics that make our world somewhat predictable, the spirit world, however, operates on a superior level that transcends our laws of physics. This makes it a little difficult to describe things such as demon possession or oppression because the spirit world is not confined to space or time. I have seen things during deliverance sessions that defy natural laws; small and frail people who required several others to help subdue them and prevent them from hurting themselves and others when evil spirits manifested in them. I have seen physical reactions and contortions that defied laws of physics and our natural realm.

I have witnessed people I have been ministering to suddenly have supernatural knowledge of things that were taking place elsewhere in other rooms at that same moment. What they said was proven to be correct and they could not have possibly known except for the demonic powers at work within them. We have to remember that the behaviour of the spirit world is difficult to define because demons are lawless and break God's spiritual laws like criminals break human ones.

In chapter one of this book I spoke about the *The Three "Tenses" of Salvation,* found in Scripture. Salvation involves what has been done, what is currently happening and what will one day take place in a Christian's life. We have been saved from the penalty of sin (justified). We are being saved from the power of sin (sanctified). One day we will be saved from the presence of sin (glorified). Therefore, while a demon (evil spirit) cannot have a Christian to possess and fully control, a Christian who is not yet glorified can still be oppressed and influenced by demonic powers and have a demon or indeed many of them operating in their life.

There are two Greek words used for oppressed in the New Testament. One is *thrauo*, it is the word Jesus uses when He says He has come to set free those who are oppressed. It means those who are crushed and broken in pieces. The other word for oppressed is the Greek word *katadunasteuo* which means to exercise power over someone, (Acts 10:38). So while a Christian cannot be possessed by demons they can be crushed, broken and under the power of them.

Possession implies ownership. This is not a word that appears anywhere in the New Testament with reference to demons or deliverance. The Greek word that is most often used is *daimonizomai* meaning demonised or demon affected and afflicted. Perhaps a more helpful word to aid our understanding of this complex issue is *infected.*

Demonization is the language of infection and not just invasion

Some argue that since light can have no fellowship with darkness (2 Corinthians 6:14), how can the Holy Spirit and an evil spirit reside in the same place – a Christian believer's life? But note the question of whether or not a Christian can be demon infected and affected is not about fellowship but presence and activity. This world is filled with both the presence of God and dark demonic powers. They cannot fellowship together but they exist together until the day God finally destroys all evil. Likewise, the Holy Spirit dwells within a believer and does not leave them every time they sin.

When the Holy Spirit comes into a believer's life their spirit is *born again* and made alive to God. They are forgiven and become a new creation positionally in Christ. They do not become instantaneously perfect and free from every effect that sin has had upon them, but now they are free to become free. They are saved to be made whole in every area of their life.

We are composed of three parts; a body, (our physical being), a soul (mind, will and emotions) and a spirit (1 Thessalonians 5:23). The spirit of a Christian belongs to God and their spirit is united with the Holy Spirit, but their bodies and souls can still be afflicted and infected by evil spirits. Just like you can turn a light on in one room and the next room in the house can be dark, the same is true in the spirit realm.

Our spirits are instantly made new the moment we are saved, but our souls can take time to renew and *clean up*. I do not believe a demon can control the spirit of a person after having accepted Jesus, but where demons do their work is in the soul and through the soul they seek to overwhelm and affect our spirit.

Derek Prince (author of *They Shall Expel Demons*) does a good job at pointing out how the Greek does not suggest that a demon can *own* a person, but rather a person can be under the *influence* of a demon.

He says, "Saying that a Christian can be possessed, is like saying that a person's body is owned by an infection on that person's finger. The infection may *influence* the body, but it does not mean that it *owns* the body. The same is true here: while a Christian can have a demon and be in bondage (influenced), it does not mean that the person is owned by the demon."

Demons can invade the life of a believer (if given the rights of course), but not the spirit (the real you), because the spirit belongs to the Lord. The soul is where your thoughts, emotions and thinking are done. Demons can cause fear, depression, lust, uncontrollable anger and other iniquities in the soul, as well as sickness and diseases in the body.

It doesn't matter who you are (whether a believer or a non-believer), if you've given the enemy rights to your soul or body, then you are up for a spiritual infection that can result in demonic bondage.

When you read through the Gospels Jesus is constantly confronting demons and demonic powers. This was among a people who were the most religious on earth. They had received more revelation from God and experienced His power more than any other nation and yet Jesus had to deal with evil spirits everywhere He went.

"But if I drive out demons by the finger of God, then the kingdom of God has come upon you," Luke 11:20.

He also taught and prepared His followers to do the same and the job description of every Christian is the same, no matter what their specific gifting and calling,

"Heal the sick, raise the dead, cleanse those who have leprosy, drive out demons. Freely you have received; freely give," Matthew 10:8.

He said to them, "Go into all the world and preach the gospel to all creation. Whoever believes and is baptized will be saved, but whoever does not believe will be condemned. And these signs will accompany those who believe: In my name they will drive out demons; they will speak in new tongues; they will pick up snakes with their hands; and when they drink deadly poison, it will not hurt them at all; they will place their hands on sick people, and they will get well."

Mark 16:15-18

...God anointed Jesus of Nazareth with the Holy Spirit and power, and how he went around doing good and healing all who were under the power of the devil, because God was with him, Acts 10:38.

As the Father has sent me, I am sending you, John 20:21.

Note that we are not told to cast *off* demons but cast them *out*. To do this they must first be within a person (infected) not just against or upon them.

If we will not minister deliverance to an unbeliever because we think they first need to give their lives to Jesus (a house swept clean of an evil spirit and not put in order attracts more evil spirits, Luke 11:24-26), and we will not minister deliverance to a Christian because we think they cannot have a demon, then who is deliverance for? The deliverance ministry is primarily for the people of God (Matthew 15:26, Luke 13:16).

If you insist that when a person becomes a Christian all demonic presence and infection automatically leave that person then why are we commanded to cast out demons? All we would need to do is lead someone to Christ.

Jesus' ministry was full of setting people free from demonic spirits and He was ministering among the most religious people on the planet.

Scholarly Comments

Dr Merrill Unger

In his treatise *Demons in the World Today*, Dr Merrill Unger writes,

"In demon influence, evil spirits exert power over a person short of actual possession. Such influence may vary from mild harassment to extreme subjection when body and mind become dominated and held in slavery by spirit agents. Christians, as well as non-Christians, can be so influenced. They may be oppressed, vexed, depressed, hindered and bound by demons."

Dr Unger is frank to say that he had written in 1952, "To demon possession, only unbelievers are exposed." Twenty years later, he writes, "This statement was inferred, since Scripture does not clearly settle the question. It was based on the assumption that an evil spirit could not indwell the redeemed body together with the Holy Spirit." Missionaries from all over the world wrote to him, telling of cases to the contrary and, as the author notes, the claims of the missionaries "appear valid."

(*What Demons Can Do To Saints* published by Moody Press)

Dr V. Raymond Edman

Dr V. Raymond Edman, president of Wheaton College from 1941-1965, wrote the following in answer to the question about Christians having a demon,

"The unguarded Christian may have demon possession in the soul, which would affect mental processes and emotions; or in the body, as was the case of the woman who had a *'spirit of infirmity eighteen years and was bowed together, and could in no wise lift up herself'* (Luke 13:11). Of her, the Saviour said when He healed her, *'Ought not this woman, being a daughter of Abraham, who Satan hath bound, lo, these eighteen years, be loosed from this bond on the Sabbath day?'* To say that a Christian cannot be demonized in any area of his life is a happy but inaccurate generalization."

Appendix 3

The Heart and the Mind

The Bible describes "the heart" as referring to the whole person. It represents our entire mental and moral activity.[1]

This is why we are told in Proverbs 4:23, *"Above all else guard your heart for from it flows the issues of life,"* and in Proverbs 27:19, *"As water reflects a face, so a man's heart reflects the man."* The heart defines who we are and influences everything we do.

The heart is the master control area of our life. What rules there shapes our thoughts, forms our attitudes and determines our actions.

The heart is also the centre of man's intellect, emotion and will. Therefore the "heart" and "mind" are sometimes used interchangeably in the Scripture. The Hebrew writer says, for example, *"This is the covenant that I will make with them after those days, says the Lord: I will put my laws upon their heart, and on their mind I will write them,"* (Hebrews 11:16).

In both the Old and New Testaments the word "heart" is used to refer to the whole of the innermost part of a person. When the writers speak about the heart, it never means merely human feelings (emotions).

The Biblical word "heart" comprises three parts,

1) The mental process (where action and reaction take place).

2) The emotions (which only process a reaction).

3) The will (discretionary, volitional, decision-making) where decisions are made between the rational and the emotive.

Strong's Dictionary

According to *Strong's Dictionary*, the Hebrew word *lebab* is rendered: "heart" "being" "breast," "comfortably," "courage," "midst," "mind," "unawares" and "understanding".

Strong's Greek Dictionary, states that the Greek word *kardia* is rendered: "heart" "the thoughts or feelings" (mind). [1]

Vine's Old Testament Dictionary

The Hebrew word *lebab* rendered "heart" is the seat of desire, inclination or will and can be the seat of the emotions. The "heart" could be regarded as the seat of knowledge and wisdom and as a synonym of "mind". This meaning often occurs when "heart" appears with the verb "to know"; *"Thus you are to know in your heart..."* (Deuteronomy 8:5, NASB); and *"...yet the Lord hath not given you a heart to perceive (know)..."* (Deuteronomy 29:4, KJV; RSV, "mind"). Solomon prayed, *"Give therefore thy servant an understanding heart to judge thy people that I may discern between good and bad..."* (1 Kings 3:9; cf. 4:29). Memory is the activity of the "heart" as in Job 22:22, *"...lay up his (God's) words in thine heart".*

Vine's New Testament Dictionary

The Greek word *kardia* is rendered "heart" (English *cardiac*), is the chief organ of physical life (*"for the life of the flesh is in the blood,"* Leviticus 17:11), and occupies the most important place in the human system. By an easy transition, the word came to stand for man's entire mental and moral activity, both the rational and the emotional elements.

In other words, the heart is used figuratively for the hidden springs of the personal life. The Bible describes human depravity as in the "heart", because sin is a principle which has its seat in the centre of man's inward life, and then "defiles" the whole circuit of his action, Matthew 15:19, 20. On the other hand, Scripture regards the heart as the sphere of divine influence, Romans. 2:15; Acts 15:9 etc.

The heart, as lying deep within, contains *"the hidden man",* 1Peter 3:4, the real man. It represents the true character but also conceals it (J. Laidlaw, in *Hastings' Bible Dictionary*). As to its usage in the New Testament it denotes (a) the seat of physical life, Acts 14:17; James 5:5; (b) the seat of moral nature and spiritual life, the seat of grief, John 14:1; Romans 9:2; 2 Corinthians 2:4; joy, John 16:22; Ephesians 5:19; the desires, Matthew 5:28; 2 Peter 2:14; the affections, Luke 24:32; Acts 21:13; the perceptions, John 12:40; Ephesians 4:18; the thoughts, Matthew 9:4; Hebrews. 4:12; the understanding, Matthew 13:15; Romans 1:21; the reasoning powers, Mark 2:6; Luke 24:38; the imagination, Luke 1:51; conscience, Acts 2:37; 1 John 3:20; the intentions, Hebrews 4:12, (cf.) 1 Peter 4:1; purpose, Acts 11:23; 2 Corinthians 9:7; the will, Romans 6:17; Colossians 3:15; faith, Mark 11:23; Romans 10:10; Hebrews 3:12. The heart, in its moral significance in the Old Testament, includes the emotions, the reason, and the will. 2

Holman Bible Dictionary

The heart is the centre of the physical, mental, and spiritual life of humans. This contrasts to the normal use of *kardia* ("heart") in Greek literature outside the Scriptures. The New Testament follows the Old Testament usage when referring to the human heart in that it gives *kardia* a wider range of meaning than it was generally accustomed to have.

First, the word heart refers to the physical organ and is considered to be the centre of the physical life. Eating and drinking are spoken of as strengthening the heart (Genesis 18:5; Judges 19:5; Acts 14:17). As the centre of physical life, the heart came to stand for the person as a whole.

The heart became the focus for all the vital functions of the body; including both intellectual and spiritual life. The heart and the intellect are closely connected, the heart being the seat of intelligence, *"For this people's heart is waxed gross…lest at any time they should…understand with their heart, and should be converted,"* (Matthew 13:15).

The heart is connected with thinking: As a person *"thinks in his heart, so is he,"* (Proverbs 23:7). To ponder something in one's heart means to consider it carefully (Luke 1:66; 2:19). "To set one's heart on" is the literal Hebrew that means to give attention to something or to worry about it (1 Samuel 9:20). To call to heart (mind) something means to remember something

(Isaiah 46:8). All of these are functions of the mind, but are connected with the heart in biblical language.

Closely related to the mind are acts of the will, acts resulting from a conscious or even a deliberate decision. Thus, 2 Corinthians 9:7, *"Every man according as he purposes in his heart, so let him give."* Ananias contrived his deed of lying to the Holy Spirit in his heart (Acts 5:4). The conscious decision is made in the heart (Romans 6:17). Connected to the will are human wishes and desires. Romans 1:24 describes how God gave them up *"through the lusts of their own hearts, to dishonour their own bodies."* David was a man after God's *"own heart"* because he would *"fulfil all"* of God's will (Acts 13:22).

Not only is the heart associated with the activities of the mind and the will, but it is also closely connected to the feelings and affections of a person. Emotions such as joy originate in the heart (Psalm 4:7; Isaiah 65:14). Other emotions are ascribed to the heart, especially in the Old Testament. Nabal's fear is described by the phrase, *"his heart died within him,"* (1 Samuel 25:37; compare Psalm 143:4). Discouragement or despair is described by the phrase *"heaviness in the heart"* which makes it stoop (Proverbs 12:25).

Again, Ecclesiastes 2:20 says, *"Therefore I went about to cause my heart to despair of all the labour which I took under the sun."* Another emotion connected with the heart is sorrow. John 16:6 says, *"...because I have said these things unto you, sorrow hath filled your heart".* Proverbs 25:20, describes sorrow as having *"a heavy heart".* The heart is also the seat of the affection of love and its opposite, hate. In the Old Testament, for example, Israel is commanded, *"You shall not hate your brother in your heart, but you shall reason with your neighbour, lest you bear sin because of him,"* Leviticus 19:17 RSV).

A similar attitude, bitter jealousy, is described in James 3:14 as coming from the heart. On the other hand, love is also based in the heart. The believer is commanded to love God *"with all your heart"* (Mark 12:30; compare Deuteronomy 6:5). Paul taught that the purpose of God's command is love which comes from a *"pure heart"* (1 Timothy 1:5).

Finally, the heart is spoken of in Scripture as the centre of the moral and spiritual life. The conscience, for instance, is associated with the heart. In fact, the Hebrew language had no word for conscience, so the word heart was often used to express this concept, *"my heart shall not reproach me so long as I live,"* (Job 27:6). The Revised Standard Version translates the word for "heart" as "conscience" in 1 Samuel 25:31 (RSV). In the New Testament the heart is spoken of also as that which condemns us (1 John 3:19-21).

All moral conditions from the highest to the lowest are said to centre in the heart. Sometimes the heart is used to represent a person's true nature or character. Samson told Delilah *"all his heart"* (Judges 16:17). This true nature is contrasted with the outward appearance, *"man looks on the outward appearance, but the Lord looks on the heart,"* 1 Samuel 16:7 RSV).

On the negative side, depravity is said to issue from the heart, *"The heart is deceitful above all things, and desperately wicked: who can know it?"* (Jeremiah 17:9). Jesus said that out of the heart comes evil thoughts, murder, adultery, fornication, theft, false witness and slander (Matthew 15:19). In other words, defilement comes from within rather than from without.

Because the heart is at the root of the problem, this is the place where God does His work in the individual. For instance, the work of the law is *"written in their hearts,"* and conscience is the proof of this (Romans 2:15). The heart is the field where seed (the Word of God) is sown (Matthew 13:19; Luke 8:15). In addition to being the place where the natural laws of God are written, the heart is the place of renewal. Before Saul became king, God gave him a new heart (1 Samuel 10:9). God promised Israel that He would give them a new spirit within, take away their *"stony heart"* and give them a *"heart of flesh"* (Ezekiel 11:19). Paul said that a person must believe in the heart to be saved, *"for with the heart man believeth unto righteousness"* (Romans 10:10). (See also Mark 11:23; Hebrews 3:12.)

Finally, the heart is the dwelling place of God. Two persons of the Trinity are said to reside in the heart of the believer. God has given us the *"Ernest of the Spirit in our hearts"* (2 Corinthians 1:22). Ephesians 3:17 expresses the desire that *"Christ may dwell in your hearts by faith."* The love of God *"is shed abroad in our hearts by the Holy Ghost which is given unto us,"* (Romans 5:5). 3

Easton's Bible Dictionary

According to the Bible, the heart is the centre not only of spiritual activity, but also of all the operations of human life. "Heart" and "soul" are often used interchangeably (Deuteronomy 6:5; 26:16; compare with Matthew 22:37; Mark 12:30, 33), but this is not generally the case. The heart is the "home of the personal life," and hence a man is designated, according to his heart, wise (1 Kings 3:12, etc.), pure (Psalm

24:4; Matthew 5:8, etc.), upright and righteous (Genesis 20:5, 6; Psalm 11:2; 78:72), pious and good (Luke 8:15), etc. In these and such passages the word soul could not be substituted for heart.

The heart is also the seat of the conscience (Romans 2:15). It is naturally wicked (Genesis 8:21), and hence it contaminates the whole life and character (Matthew 12:34;15:18; compare Ecclesiastes 8:11; Psalm 73:7). Hence, the heart must be changed, regenerated (Ezekiel 36:26; 11:19; Psalm 51:10-14), before a man can willingly obey God. The process of salvation begins in the heart by the believing reception of the testimony of God, while the rejection of that testimony hardens the heart (Psalm 95:8; Proverbs 28:14; 2 Chronicles 36:13). 4

The heart is the focus and determination of the mind, and the response of the emotions. The Bible never instructs us to be led by our emotions, but rather by our minds. It is with our minds that we focus our attention and choose to obey God, and it is those actions that first are decided with our mind in consideration of what we focus on – that is what God holds us accountable for.

1.   STRONG'S EXHAUSTIVE CONCORDANCE TOGETHER WITH DICTIONARIES OF HEBREW AND GREEK WORDS, James Strong, Baker Book House Company, Grand Rapids, MI 49546, USA, 1981, electronic media.

2.   VINE'S EXPOSITORY DICTIONARY OF OLD AND NEW TESTAMENT WORDS, W.E. Vine, Ellis Enterprises Inc., Oklahoma City, OK 73120, USA, 1988, electronic media.

3.   HOLMAN BIBLE DICTIONARY, General Editor: Trent C. Butler, PH. D., Gerald Cowen, Holman Bible Publishers, Nashville, TE 37234, USA, electronic media.

4.   EASTON'S BIBLE DICTIONARY AND BOOK SYNOPSIS, Easton, M.G., Ellis Enterprises Inc., Oklahoma City, OK 73120, USA, 1988-1999, electronic media.

Other books by
David Holdaway

The Life of Jesus

The Life of Jesus More Than A prophet

Never Enough

Money and Spiritual Warfare

Surviving and Succeeding in a Financial Crisis

Was Jesus Rich?

How to Stand Against a Spiritual Attack

No More Fear

Winning Over Worry

The Wonder of Christmas

Jesus The Wonder of Christmas

The Captured Heart

The Burning Heart

Issues of the Heart

Revival is a Heart Issue

What Word do all University Professors Spell Wrong?

They Saw Jesus

Life Changing Insights From the World's Most famous Song: Psalm 23

Footholds and Strongholds

How to Know The Will of God

All these books are available in good book
shops and also by contacting the author

Davidholdaway1@aol.com

For more information on David Holdaway
go to: www.lifepublications.org.uk

Tel: +44 (0) 1685 371748

257